Anne-Marie Bodson
Josette Vinas y Roca

Transfer Designs
for Embroidery

Search Press

First published in Great Britain 2007 by Search Press Limited, Wellwood, North Farm Road, Tunbridge Wells, Kent TN2 3DR

Originally published in France 2006 by
Le Temps Apprivoisé (LTA), 7, rue des Canettes, 75006, Paris

Original title *Transferts pour nappes – vol 2*

Copyright © 2006, LTA, a division of Meta-Éditions
Dépôt legal: April 2006

English translation by Ian West in association with First Edition Translations Ltd, Cambridge, UK

English translation copyright © Search Press Limited 2007

ISBN 10: 1-84448-241-3

ISBN 13: 978-1-84448-241-2

All rights reserved. No part of this book, text, photographs or illustrations may be reproduced or transmitted in any form or by any means by print, photoprint, microfilm, microfiche, photocopier, internet or in any way known or as yet unknown, or stored in a retrieval system, without written permission obtained beforehand from Search Press.

English text typeset by GreenGate Publishing Services, Tonbridge, Kent
Layout: Colin de Graaff
Photogravure: Chromo 2

INTRODUCTION

The transfers in this book are aimed both at beginners and at more experienced embroiderers. Whatever your standard, you should be able to adapt them to make exquisite original designs.

We suggest a variety of designs in many different styles: they will look terrific on cushions, pillow slips, bags, wallhangings and accessories.

If possible, use cotton or linen, which are much easier to work with than silk or velvet. Detailed designs are best reserved for fine, closely woven materials, rather than loose weaves. That is not to say, however, that different fabrics cannot be beautifully embroidered. A word of caution: the material must be a light colour for the transfer show up.

APPLYING A TRANSFER

- Start by trying out a small design that you do not intend to embroider.
- Lay some paper on the ironing board to protect it, as the transfer may penetrate the material.
- Switch the iron to the 'wool' setting; do not use steam.
- Place the material on the ironing board, right side (where applicable) uppermost.
- Cut out the transfer pattern, leaving some paper round the edges. Position it with the printed side in contact with the material. Secure the pattern with sticky tape or pins.
- Press for a few seconds at a time with the iron. Do not move the iron, or you will dislodge the transfer.
- Lift the edge of the transfer and check the image. If it looks unsatisfactory, iron again.

As a rule, the same transfer can be used from three to eight times, depending on the thickness of the material. However, if treated very carefully, it can sometimes be used up to a dozen times on normal materials.

Preparing the fabric

- Wash and iron the fabric. Fold it into two and then into four to find the middle. Mark the folds by pressing with your hand.
- Decide in advance where you want the transfers. Mark their positions with French chalk or an erasable fabric marker, or even by cutting out and pinning bits of paper where required. The folds in the material will help you to line things up.

Embroidery tips

- The following pages contain suggestions for embroidering designs, but there is nothing to stop you using other types of stitching, if you prefer.
- Designs with colours embroidered in satin stitch can be made up equally well using stem stitch.
- You can also vary the colours, especially if the background material is different from the one in our pattern.
- Experiment with various numbers of strands of DMC Mouliné thread for the best result.
- Use a frame or hoop. Do not position the wooden part of the frame in the middle of an embroidery design, which would spoil it. The design must be entirely inside the hoop.

Care of materials

- If you have embroidered your design on cotton or linen using the yarns we suggest, wash it in warm, soapy water. It will not be harmed by machine washing, provided that you enclose it in a bag or pillow case.
- Always iron on the reverse side, laying the embroidered sections on cotton fleece to preserve the relief effect. Spraying a little starch in the right places will lend the work a better finish.

BASIC STITCHES

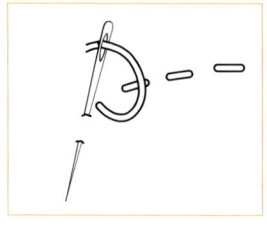

Running stitch
Work from right to left, passing the needle alternately under and over the material.

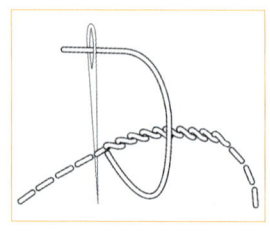

Whipped running stitch
After making a series of running stitches, pass a second thread through each, always entering at the top without piercing the material.

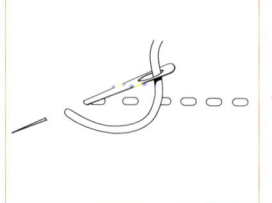

Prickstitch (spaced backstitch) (used here for isolated stitches)
The needle is drawn from the back to the front of the material and re-enters to the right-hand side of the exit point.

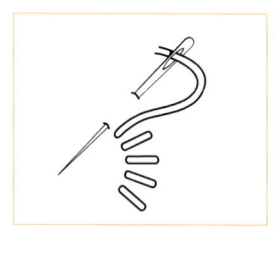

Straight stitch
A long backstitch, used in series or isolation, sometimes running in different directions.

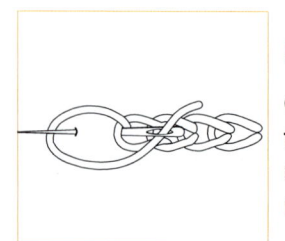

Chain stitch
Can be worked from top to bottom or right to left. Draw the needle from the back to the front, thread it back through the hole and pull to the reverse side, maintaining a loop. The needle emerges in the middle of the loop before being returned through the exit hole.

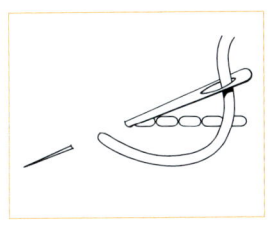

Backstitch

A series of regular prickstitches running from right to left. The thread is taken back through the previous exit hole.

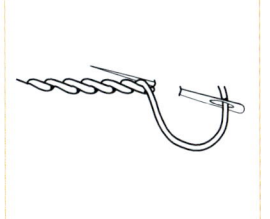

Stem stitch

A form of backstitch sewn right to left or vice versa. The needle enters the material in the middle of the previous stitch, without crossing the thread, and always on the same side of it (top or bottom).

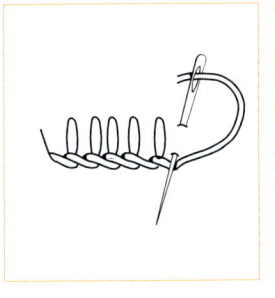

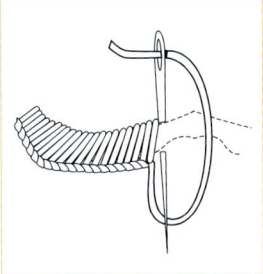

Blanket stitch and buttonhole stitch

Both types are worked from left to right. Insert and withdraw the needle vertically, and pass the thread under the needle, keeping it in place with the left thumb and pulling.
Repeat the procedure. Blanket stitch is loosely spaced; buttonhole stitch is more compact.

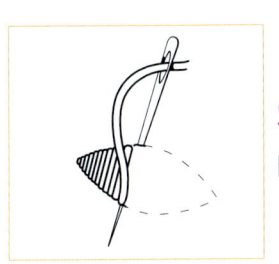

Satin stitch

Regular and parallel series of straight stitch, close together, adaptable to all surfaces.

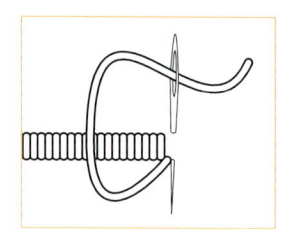

Bourdon stitch

Before employing this form of stitch – a type of satin stitch – embroider a series of running stitches to pad out the work.

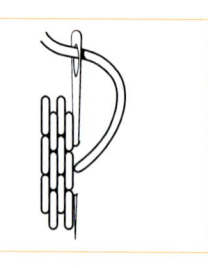

Long and short stitch/silk shading

Proceed as for the satin stitch, but using alternate long and short stitches. Change the colours at each row for a graduated effect.

French knot

Bring the needle from back to front. Make a flat loop with the thread, pass the needle through the centre of the loop and thread it back through the same hole.

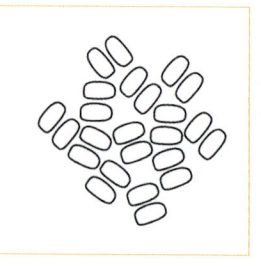

Seeding stitch

This type of fill stitching consists of identical pairs of small stitches set close together, running in all directions.

DESIGNS

Dragons

- Stitches used: satin stitch, backstitch.
- Yarn: DMC Mouliné Special 25, two strands.
- Three shades: brown 920, orange 946, orange 741.

Finished design: see page 29

Transfers pages 33–36

Delft

- Stitches used: satin stitch, stem stitch, backstitch, long and short stitch.
- Yarn: DMC Mouliné Special 25, two strands.
- Six shades: blue 796, light blue 799, blue 813, pale blue 3756, pale blue 162, green 598.

Four corner motifs are used to embellish the central design.

Finished design: see page 29

Transfers pages 37–40

India

- Stitch used: satin stitch.
- Yarn: DMC Mouliné Special 25, two strands.
- Five shades: violet 155, deep violet 3607, brown 779, pink 3706, green 954.

Finished design:
see page 29

Transfers pages 41–44

Africa

- Stitches used: satin stitch, long and short stitch, backstitch.
- Yarn: DMC Mouliné Special 25, two strands.
- Five shades: light brown 3064, brown 632, brown 437, orange 920, black 310.

Finished design: see page 30

Transfers pages 52–60

Blue faience

- Stitches used: backstitch, satin stitch, long and short stitch.
- Yarn: DMC Mouliné Special 25, two strands.
- Shade: blue 519.

Transfers pages 61–64

13

White flowers and leaves

- Stitches used: chain stitch, seeding stitch, buttonhole stitch, stem stitch.
- Yarn: DMC Mouliné Special 25, three strands.
- Two shades: white, yellow 922.

Fill the small spaces using seeding stitch in a denser pattern than in the design on pages 69–73.

Finished design: see page 30

Transfers pages 69–73

Honeysuckle

- Stitches used: satin stitch, long and short stitch, stem stitch, French knots, backstitch.
- Yarn: DMC Mouliné Special 25, two strands (but three for embroidered stems).
- Ten shades: green 907, green 94, green 3347, green 3345, brown 831, brown 371, yellow 727, yellow 444, yellow 972, violet 550.

Finished design:
see page 30

Transfers pages 45–49

Oriental dancers

- Stitches used: satin stitch, long and short stitch, stem stitch.
- Yarn: DMC Mouliné Special 25, two strands.
- Four shades: black 310, red 498, yellow 972, blue 311.

The small frieze in the middle of page 116 can be used to complete this design.

Finished design:
see page 30

Transfers pages 136–137

White alphabet

- Stitches used: satin stitch, bourdon stitch, long and short stitch, backstitch, stem stitch.
- Yarn: DMC Mouliné Special 25, three strands.
- Three shades: white, yellow 471, green 369.

Transfers pages 76–84

Climbing plants

- Stitches used: satin stitch, long and short stitch, backstitch.
- Yarn: DMC Mouliné Special 25, two strands.
- Seven shades for the vine: green 734, green 531, green 469, green 907, yellow 194, yellow 834, yellow 973.

Other climbing plants are included in the final design: wisteria, mauve-blue; passion flowers, purple; clematis, blue.

When arranging the plants, you can either mix two species together, or opt for one or the other. You could, for example, have a design with a mixture of wisteria and vine, or only clematis. The interlacing produces a heart shape: the plants should be set out either to form a rectangle/square with a heart in each corner, or with the hearts pointing to the centre of the design.

Finished design: see page 29

Transfers pages 85–92

Ancient China: by the lake

- Stitches used: satin stitch, long and short stitch, stem stitch, backstitch.
- Yarn: DMC Mouliné Special 25, two strands (but three for outlines and face features).
- Eight shades: green 3012, green 3053, green 371, green 3023, grey 822, black 310, pink 957, red 347.

Finished design:
see page 30

Transfers pages 93–100

Geometry

- Stitches used: satin stitch, long and short stitch.
- Yarn: DMC Mouliné Special 25, two strands.
- Four shades: turquoise blue 3486, dark orange 946, yellow 307, red 221.

Finished design:
see page 29

Transfers pages 65–68

Sparkling knots

- Stitch used: whipped running stitch.
- Yarn: DMC Mouliné Special 25, yellow 108, three strands, Mouliné metallic 5284, two strands.

Metallic threads have a tendency to cling to the fabric. Used as described here, however, they work like magic…

Start by embroidering the complete design in running stitch using the yellow thread. Then whip with the metallic thread.

Finished design:
see page 30

Transfers pages 101–104

Fairies

- Stitches used: satin stitch, long and short stitch, stem stitch, backstitch, French knot, prickstitch, straight stitch.
- Yarn: DMC Mouliné Special 25, three strands.
- Eight shades: pink 603, purple 917, mauve 209, blue 340, blue 792, yellow 725, orange 947, red 666.

Once the motifs have been cut out, arrange the fairies in a circle/oval border, or as a pattern. This design is also suitable for a young girl's pillow slip.

Transfers pages 105–109

Bouquets for all seasons

- Stitches used: satin stitch, long and short stitch, stem stitch, backstitch.
- Yarn: DMC Mouliné Special 25, two strands.
- Fifteen shades: blue 793, blue 796, white, green 703, green 700, orange 900, orange 742, orange 721, yellow 725, red 3350, pink 602, pink 604, pink 961, red 666, grey 452.

Each bouquet, in the form of a quarter-circle, represents one season, so you could combine the four quarters to form a complete circular arrangement, representing a year.

Finished design: see page 29

Transfers pages 112–113

Cornflowers

- Stitches used: satin stitch, long and short stitch.
- Yarn: DMC Mouliné Special 25, two strands.
- Four shades: blue 794, blue 792, green 470, green 905.

Transfer page 116

Birds on a rowan tree

- Stitches used: satin stitch, long and short stitch, stem stitch, backstitch.
- Yarn: DMC Mouliné Special 25, two strands.
- Twelve shades: green 907, green 905, green 3345, brown-green 733, black 310, red 321, red 892, blue 518, blue-grey 932, olive green, 831, yellow 727, grey 931.

The two parts of the design combine to form a square. Repeat this square several times for large designs. For example, you could use three squares in a row, or four squares forming a bigger square.

Transfers pages 117–120

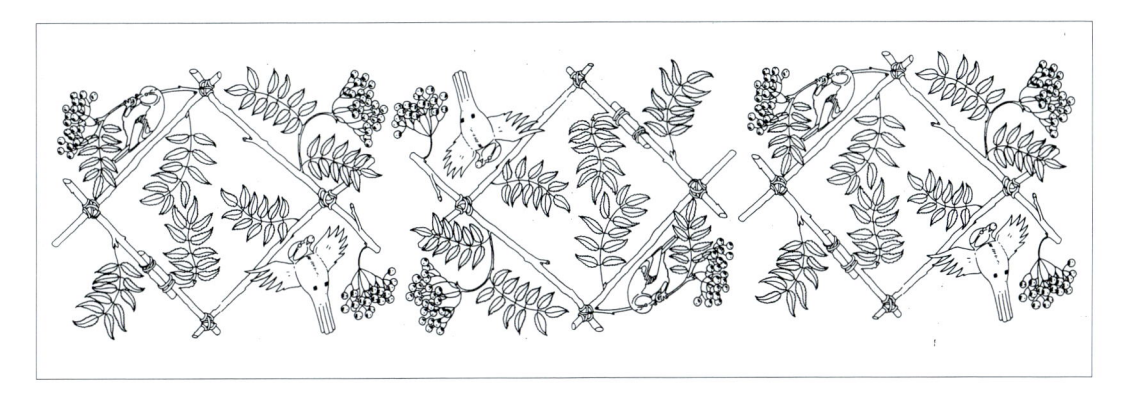

Christmas

- Stitches used: satin stitch, long and short stitch, stem stitch, backstitch.
- Yarn: DMC Mouliné Special 25, two strands.
- Seven shades: green 703, green 700, green 369, pink 304, pink 602, red 666, red 349.

Compose your own arrangement, adding in motifs (elves, holly sprays) between the structured bands. The result will be an elegant design for the festive season.

Transfers pages 121–128

Floral heart

- Stitches used: satin stitch, long and short stitch, stem stitch, French knot.
- Yarn: DMC Mouliné Special 25, two strands.
- Ten shades: blue 340, blue 796, blue 798, green 905, green 907, green 733, yellow 725, yellow 972, pink 604, grey 452.

When completed, the heart motif either occurs twice, point to point, or as four separate items in the centre of the fabric. The clusters of flowers either link the hearts or form a border. Decide where to add the insects.

Finished design: see page 29

Transfers pages 140–144

Horn of plenty

- Stitches used: satin stitch, long and short stitch, stem stitch, backstitch, French knots.
- Yarn: DMC Mouliné Special 25, two strands.
- Nine shades: orange 721, yellow 725, blue 340, pink 3787, pink 760, green 781, green 469, green 3348, grey 3023.

**Finished design:
see page 30**

Transfers pages 129–133

Finished designs

India

Dragons

Geometry

Bouquets for all seasons

Delft

Floral heart

Climbing plants

29

Horn of plenty

Oriental dancers

Ancient China: by the lake

White flowers and leaves

Sparkling knots

Honeysuckle

Africa

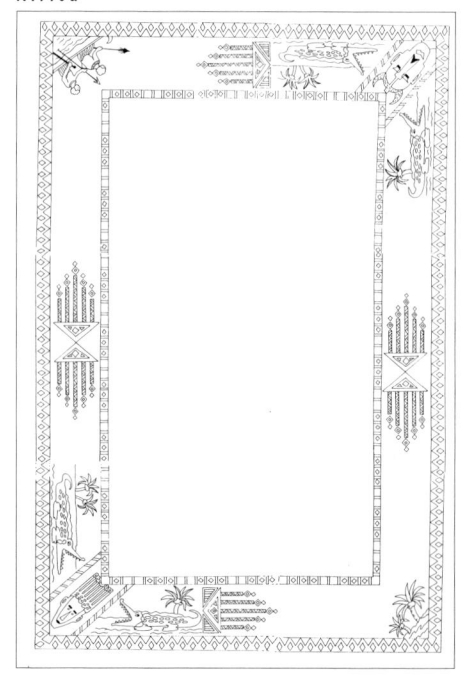

30

CONTENTS

Introduction	3
Applying a transfer	4
Preparing the fabric	4
Embroidery tips	5
Care of materials	5
Basic stitches	6
Designs	9

LIST OF TRANSFERS in alphabetical order

Africa, pages 52–60
Ancient China: by the lake, pages 93–100
Birds on a rowan tree, pages 117–120
Blue faience, pages 61–64
Bouquets for all seasons, pages 112–13
Christmas, pages 121–128
Climbing plants pages 85–92
Cornflowers, page 116
Delft, pages 37–40
Dragons, pages 33–36
Fairies, pages 105–109
Floral heart, pages 140–144
Geometry pages 65–68
Honeysuckle, pages 45–49
Horn of plenty, pages 129–133
India, pages 41–44
Oriental dancers, pages 136–137
Sparkling knots, pages 101–104
White alphabet, pages 76–84
White flowers and leaves, pages 69–73

Transfers

33

36

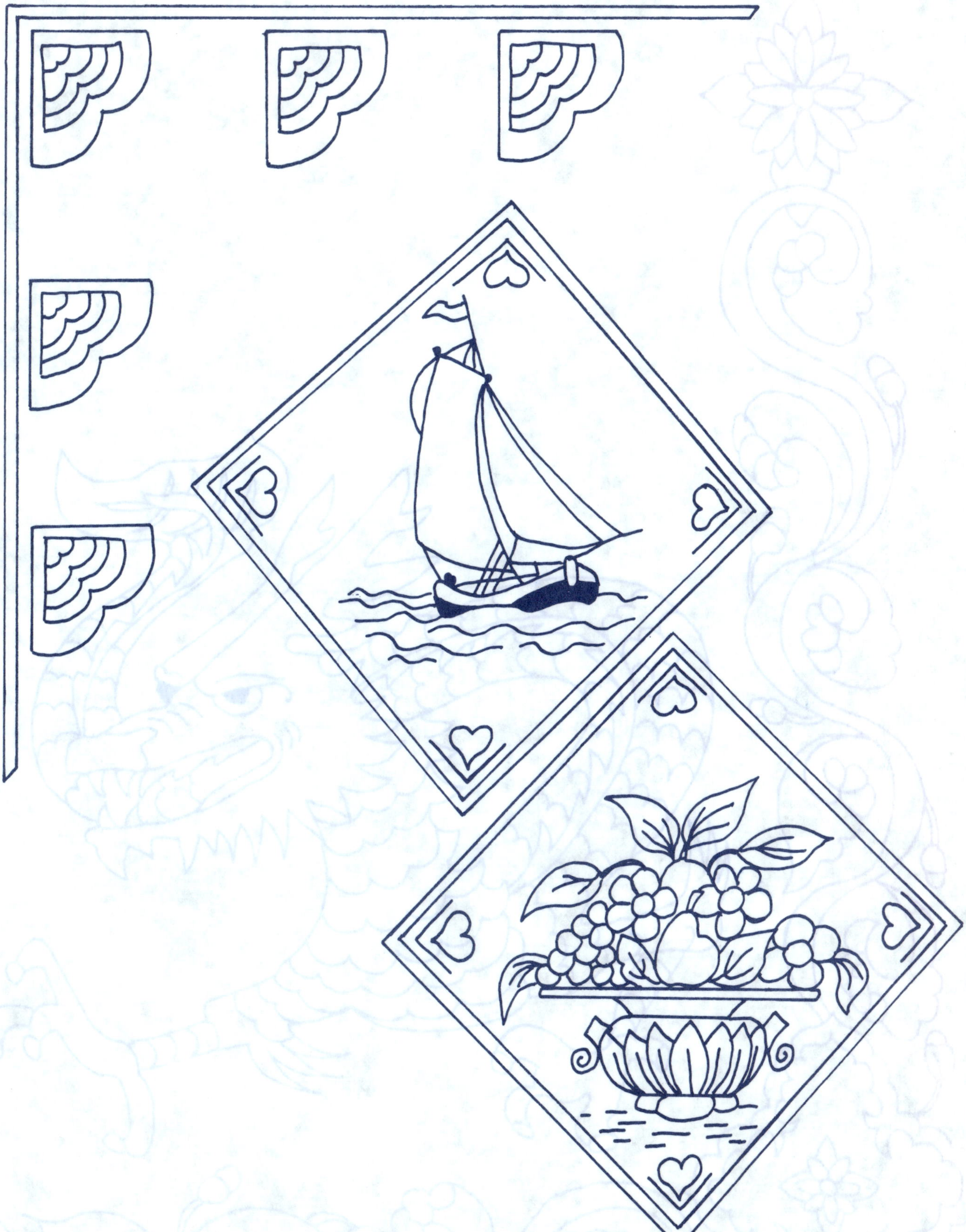

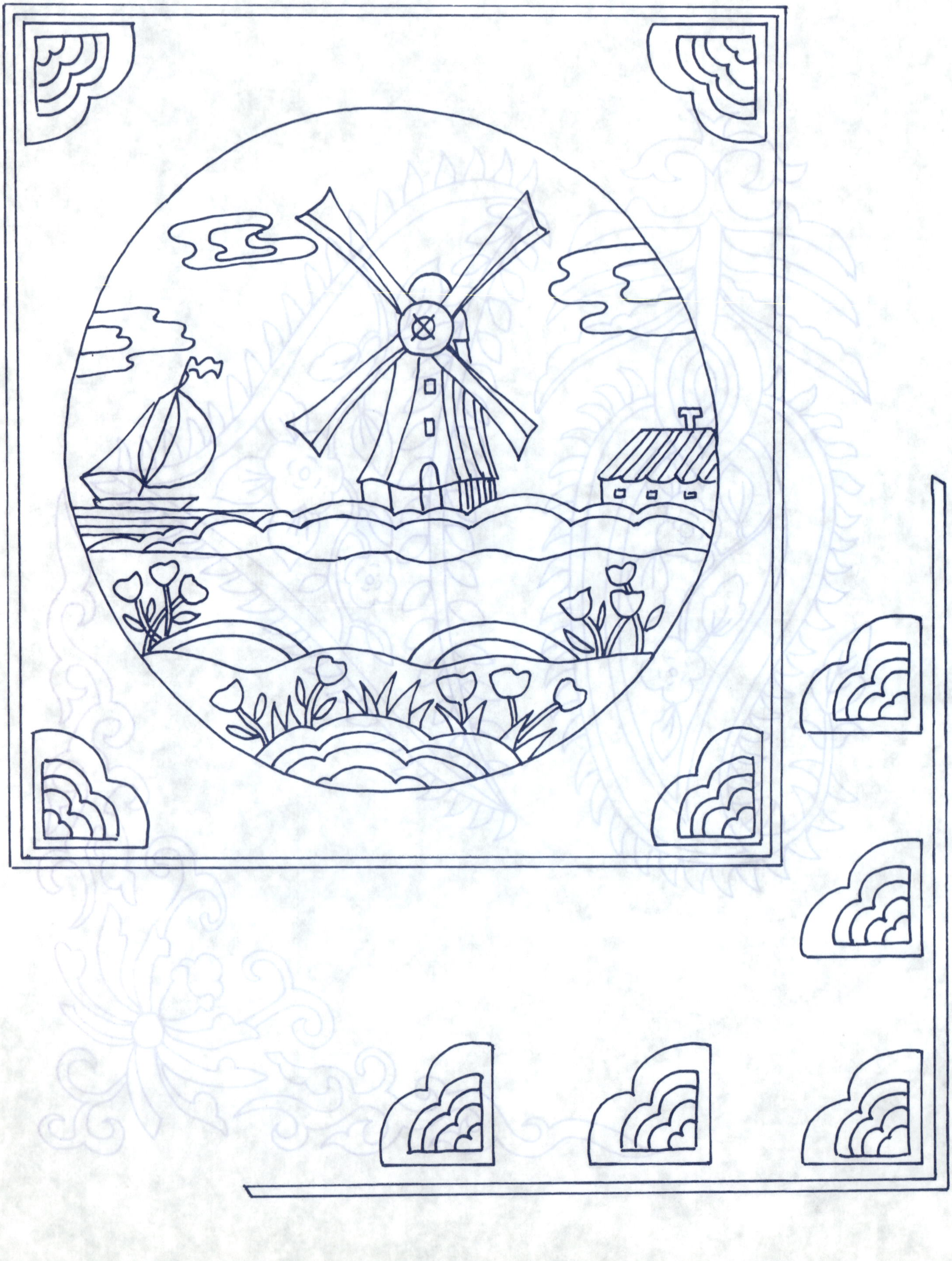

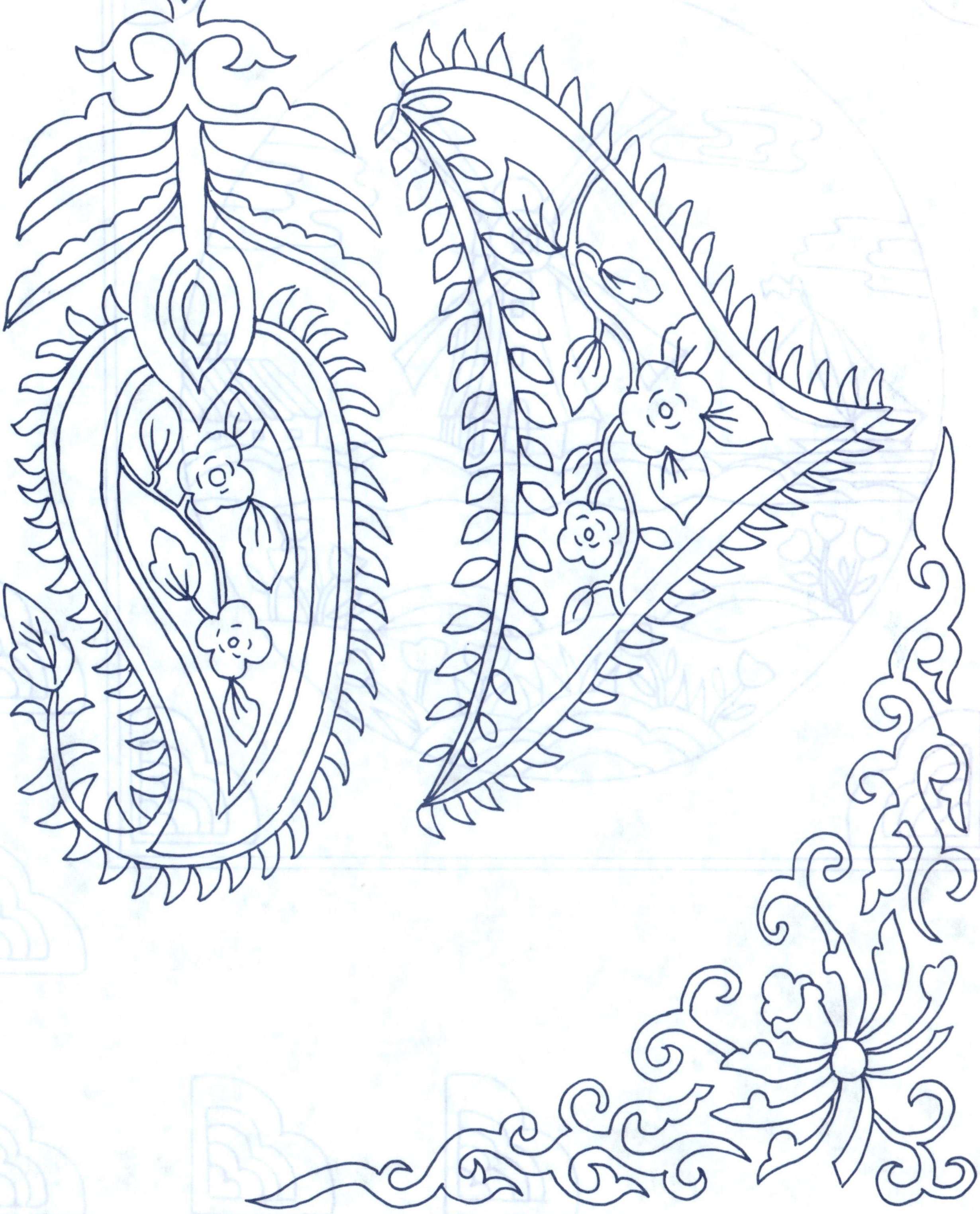

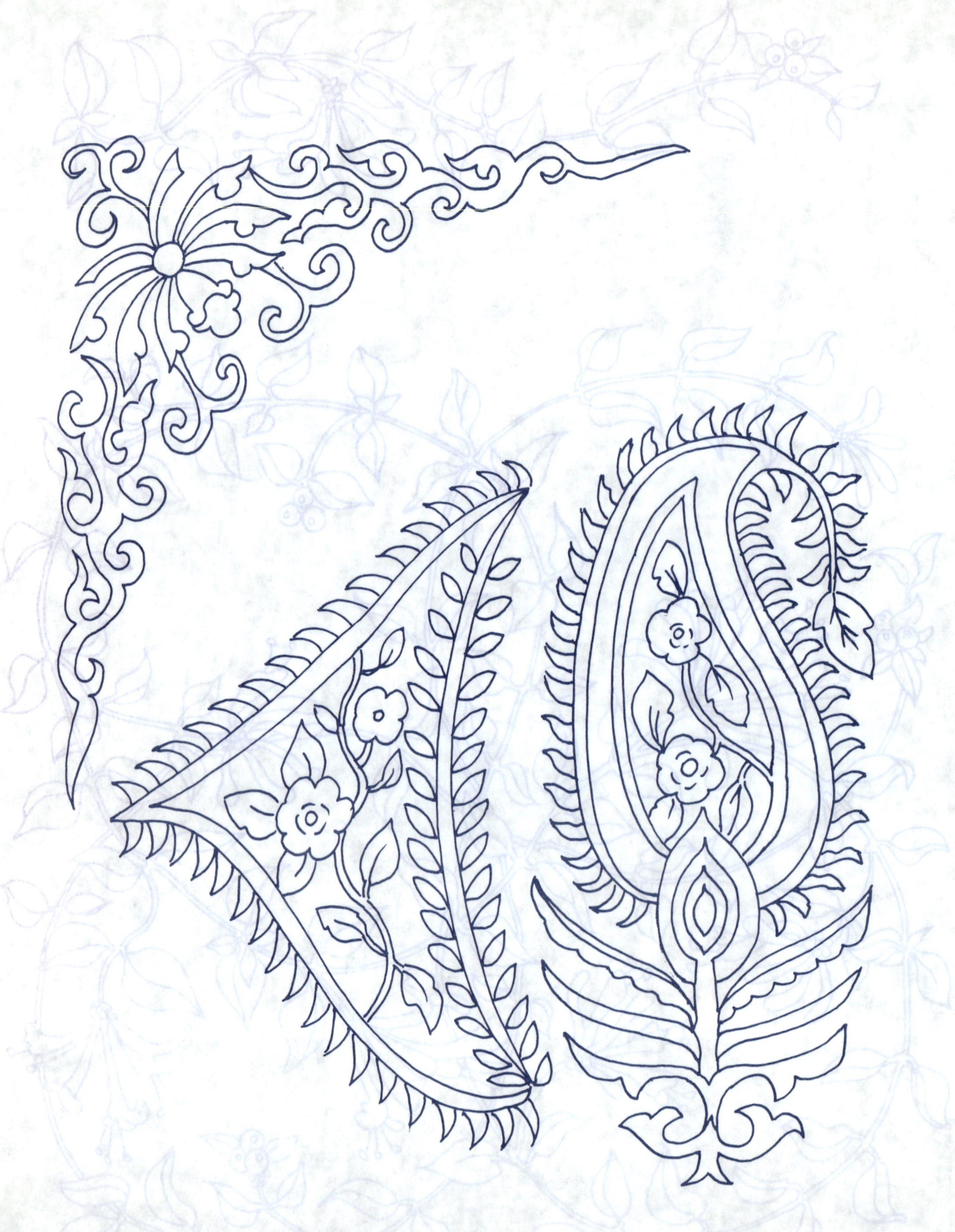

45

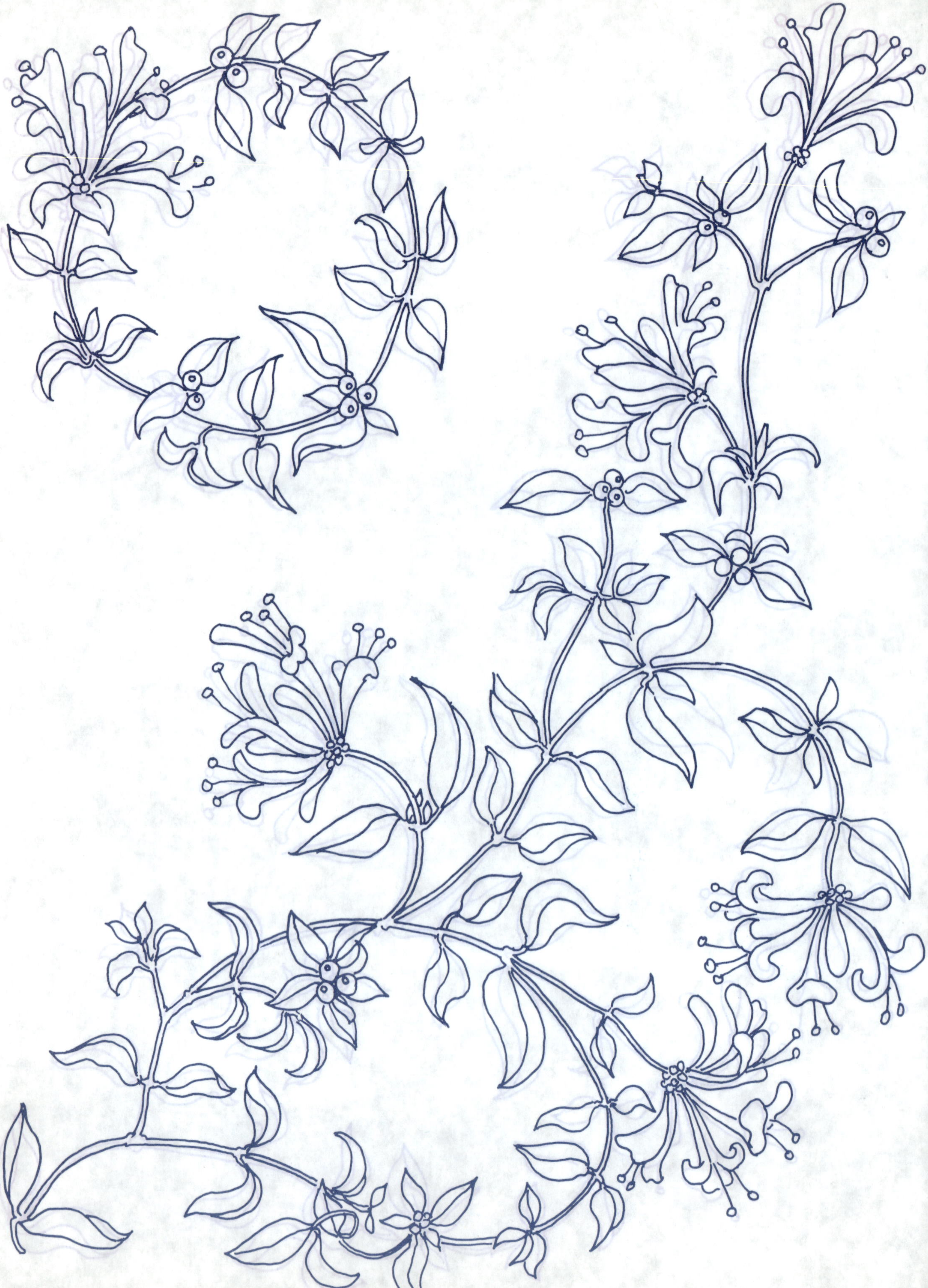

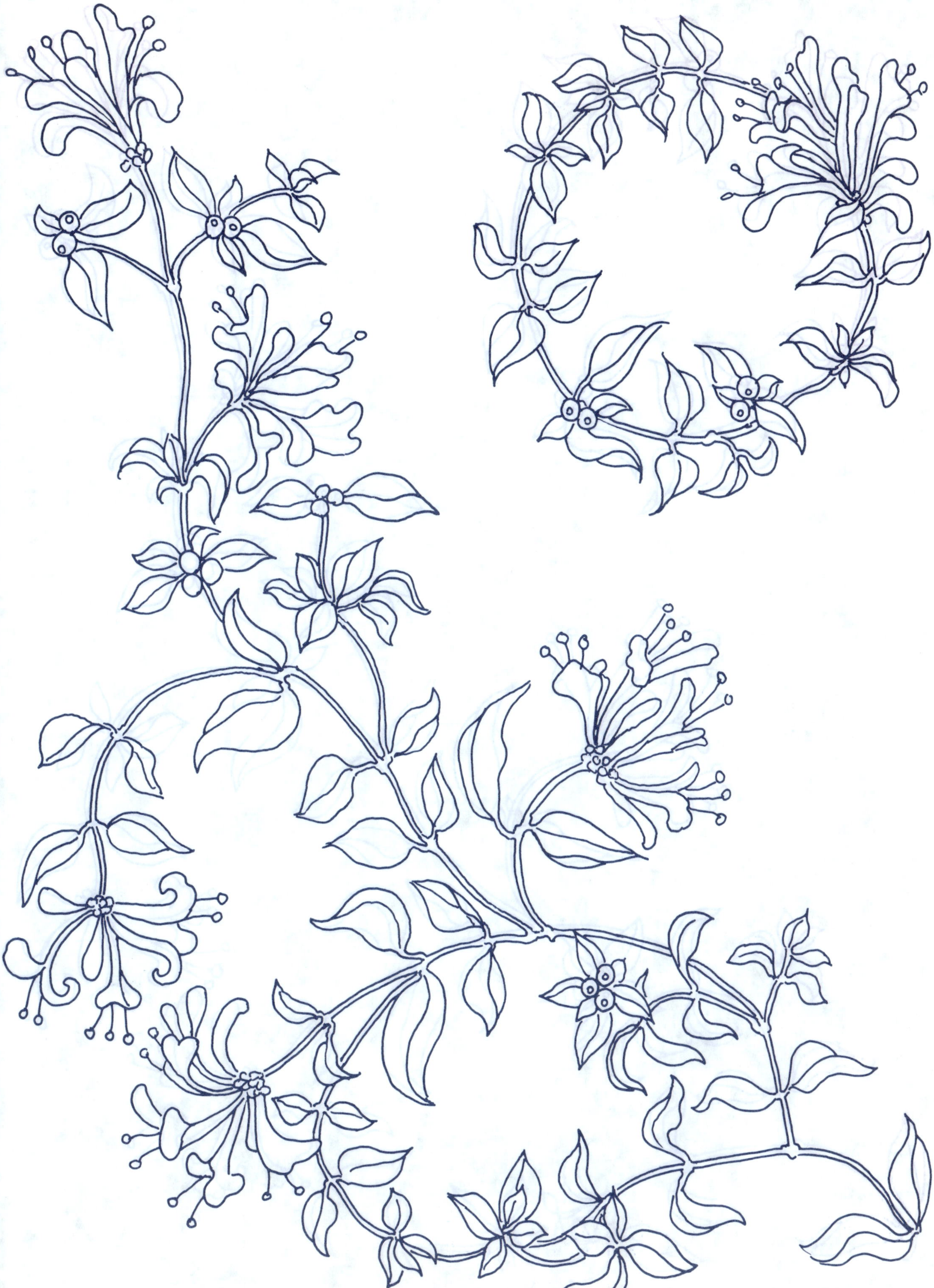

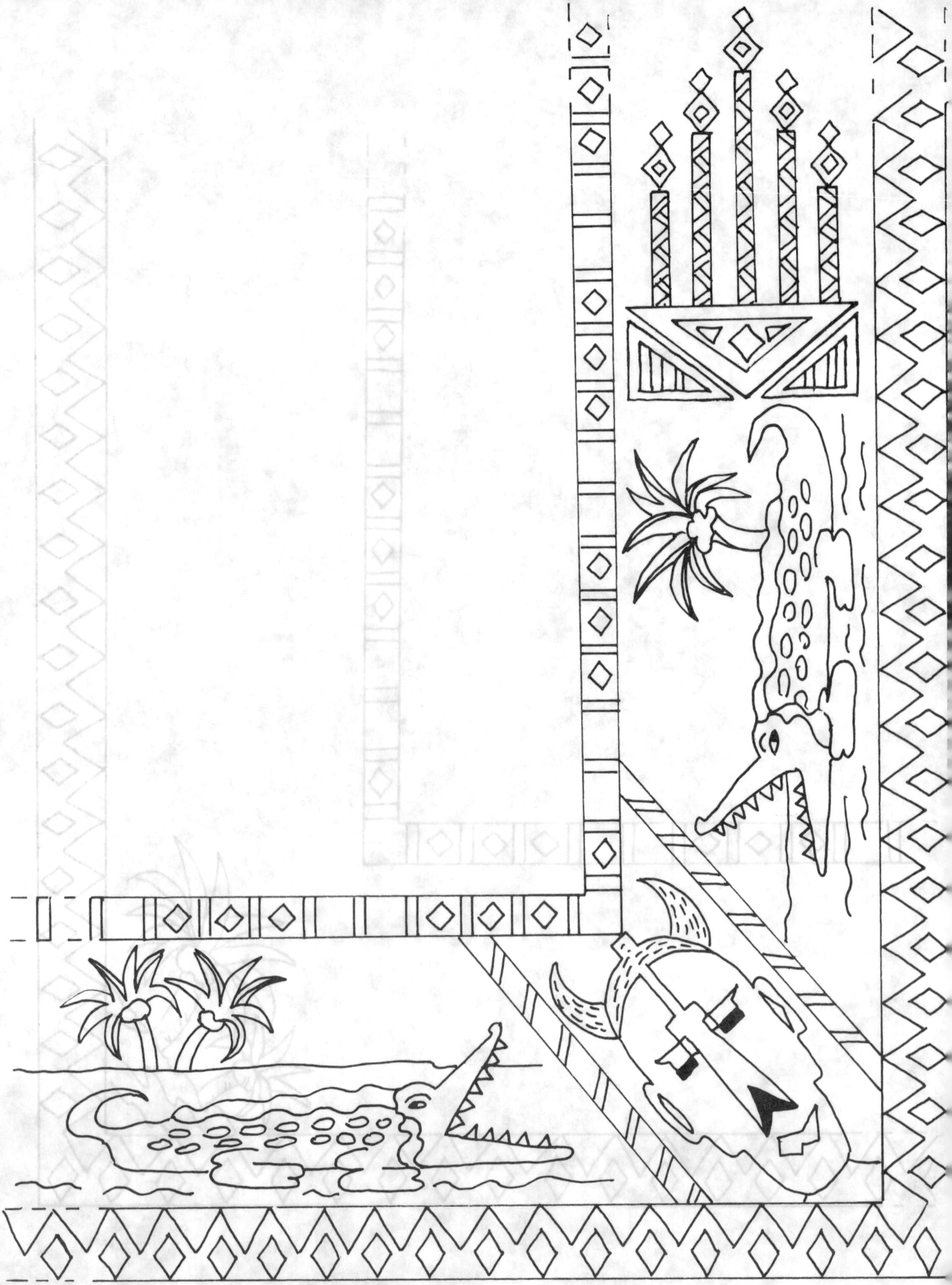

53

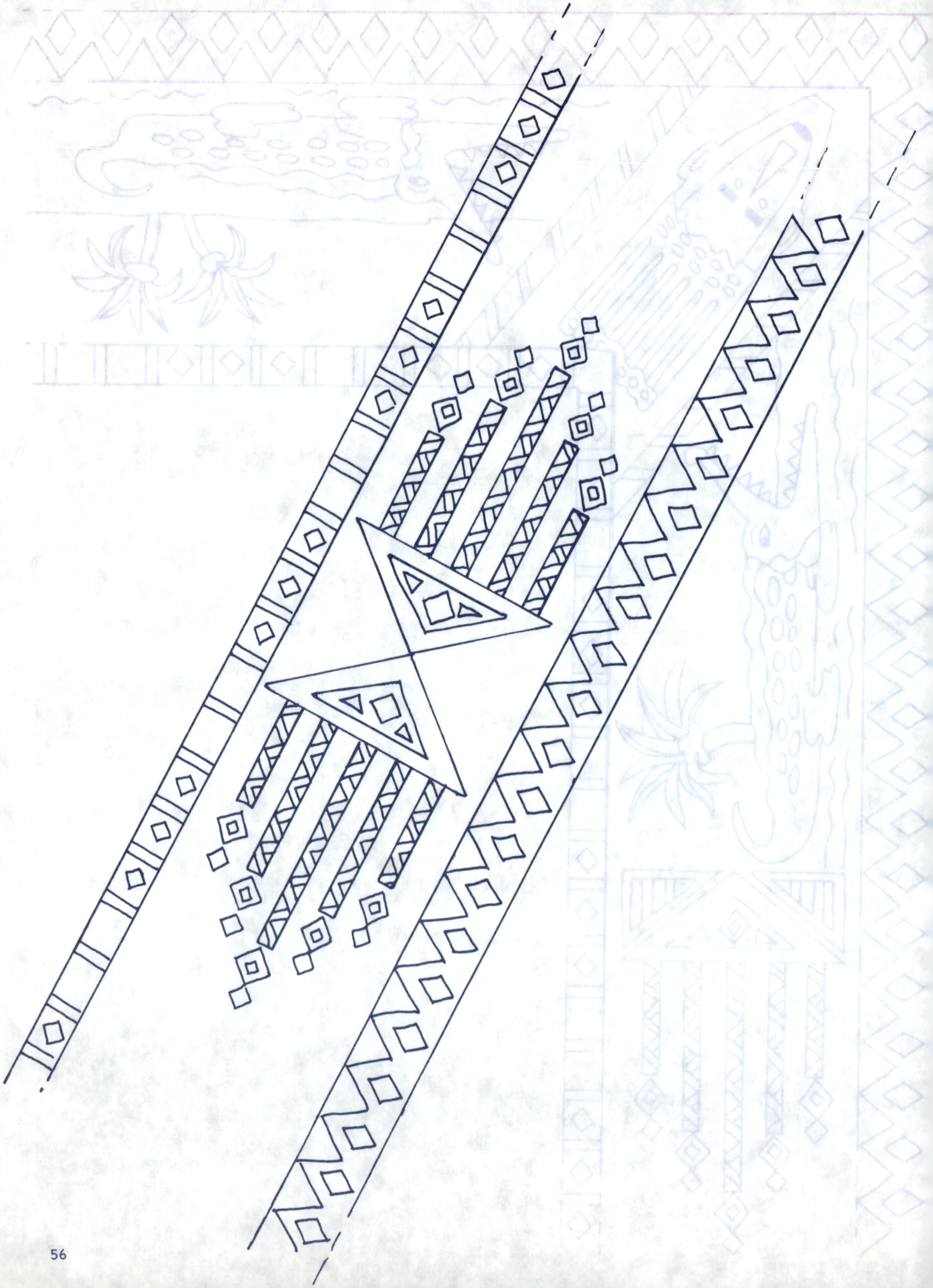

57

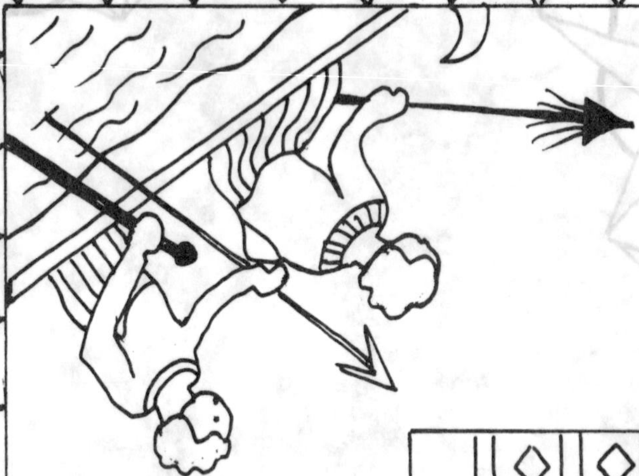

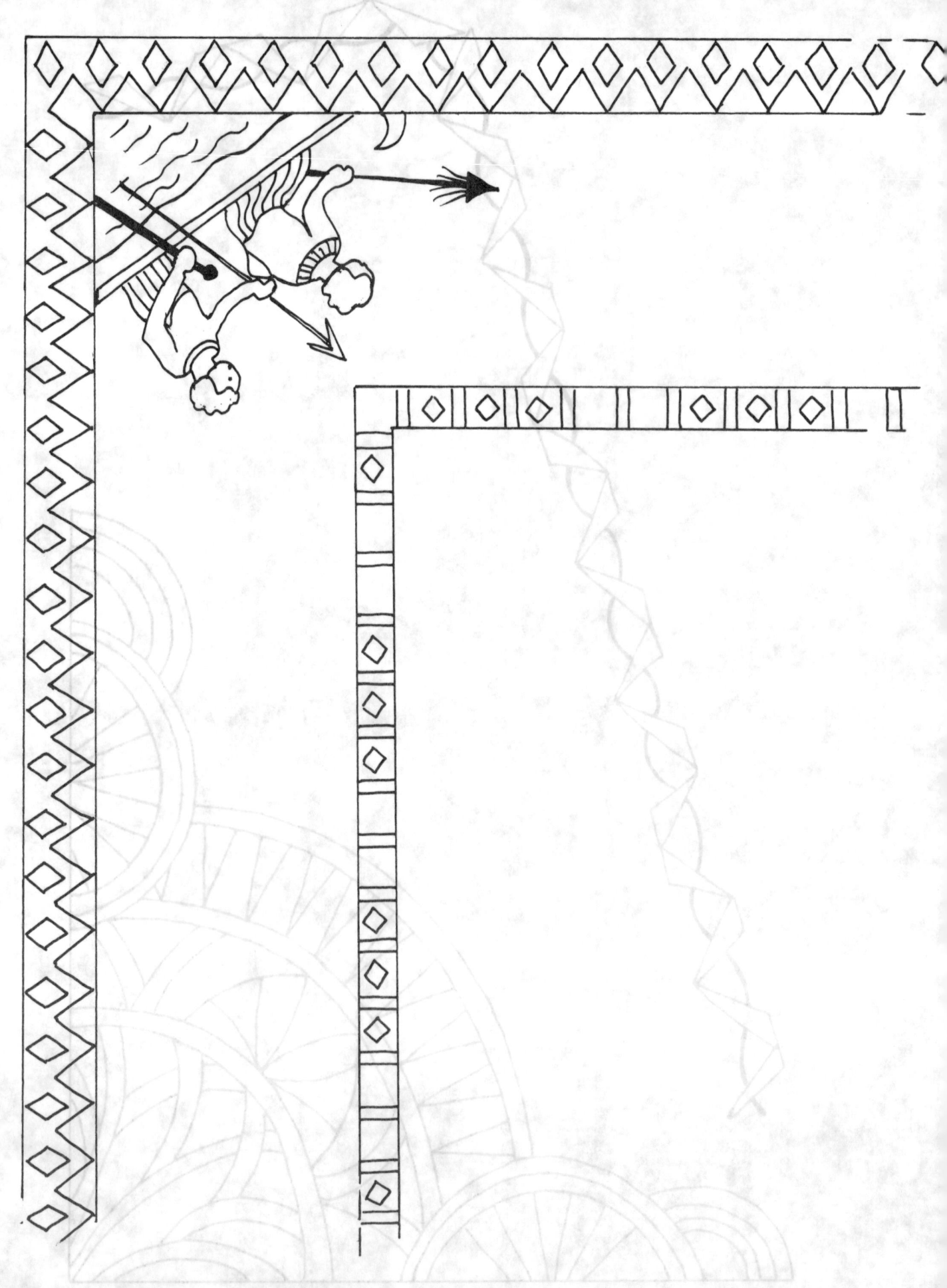

61

64

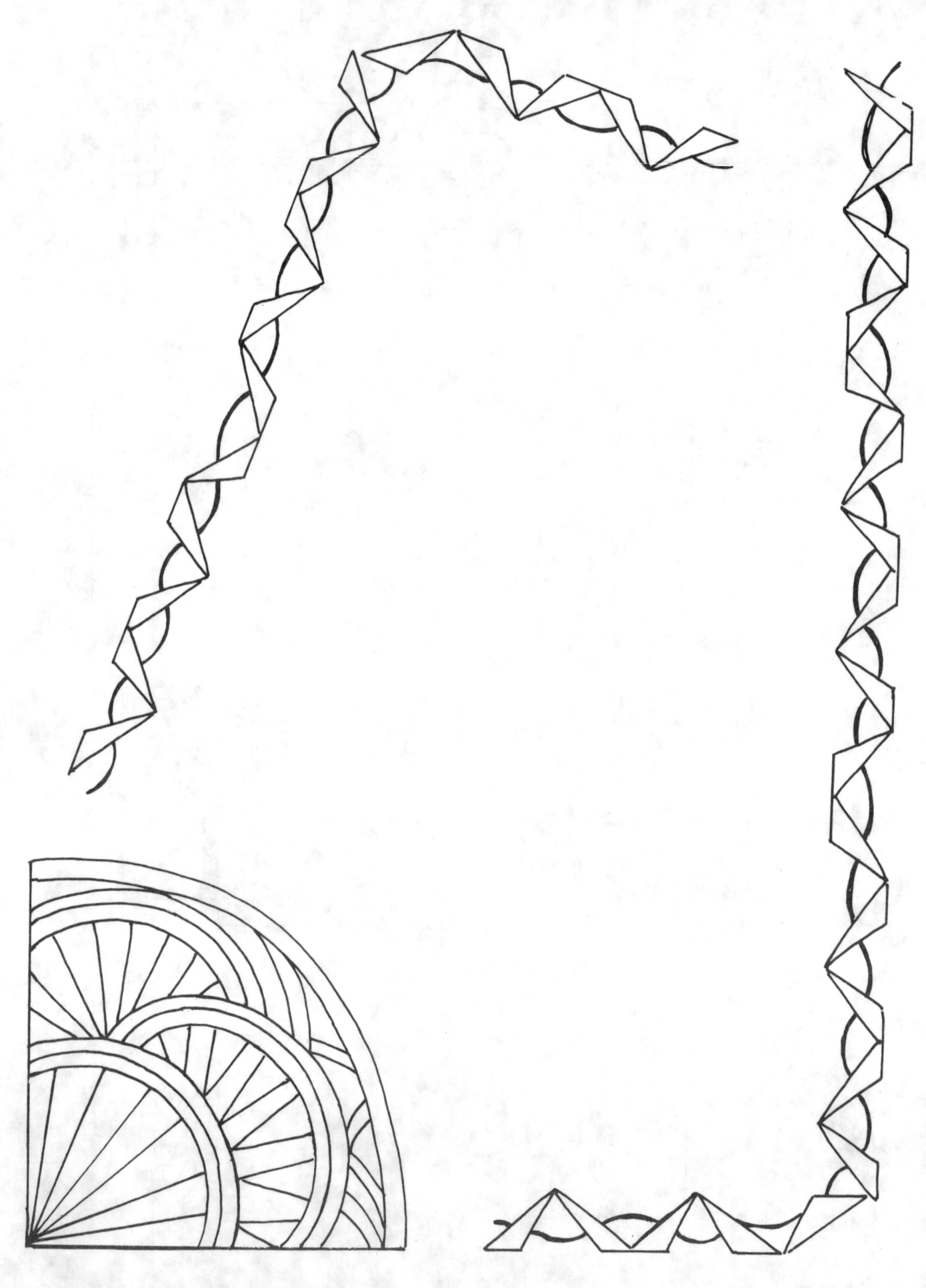

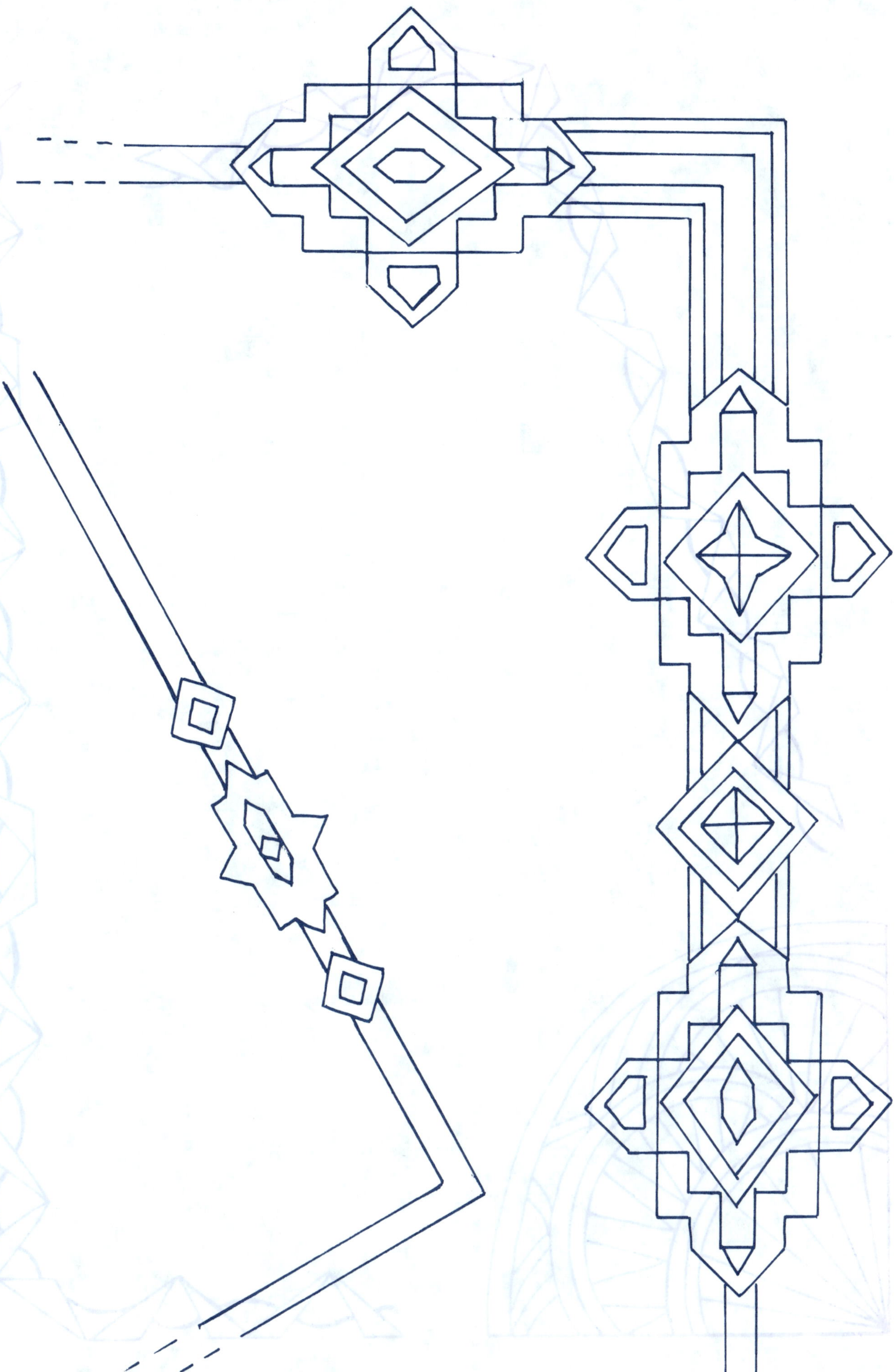

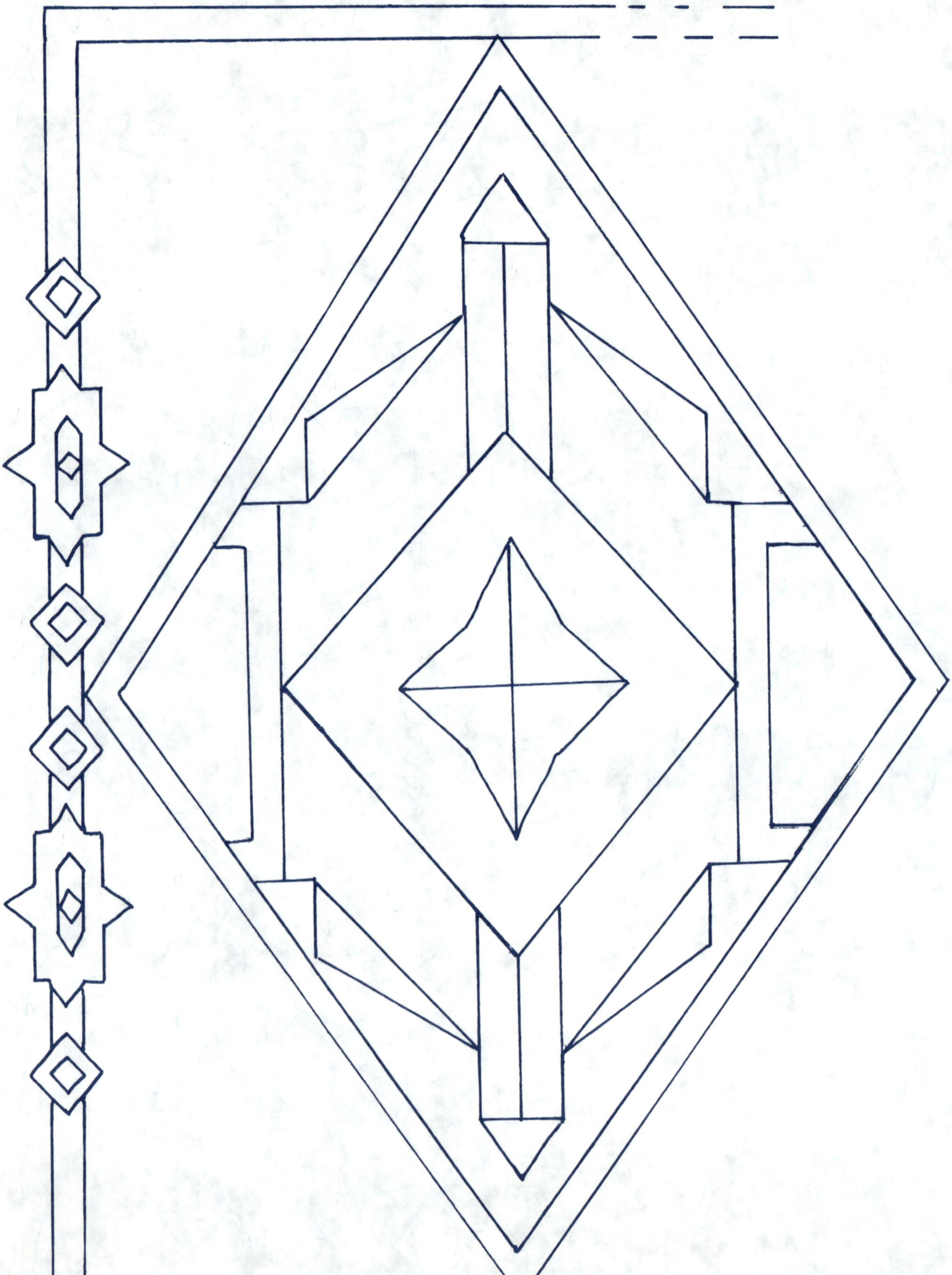

69

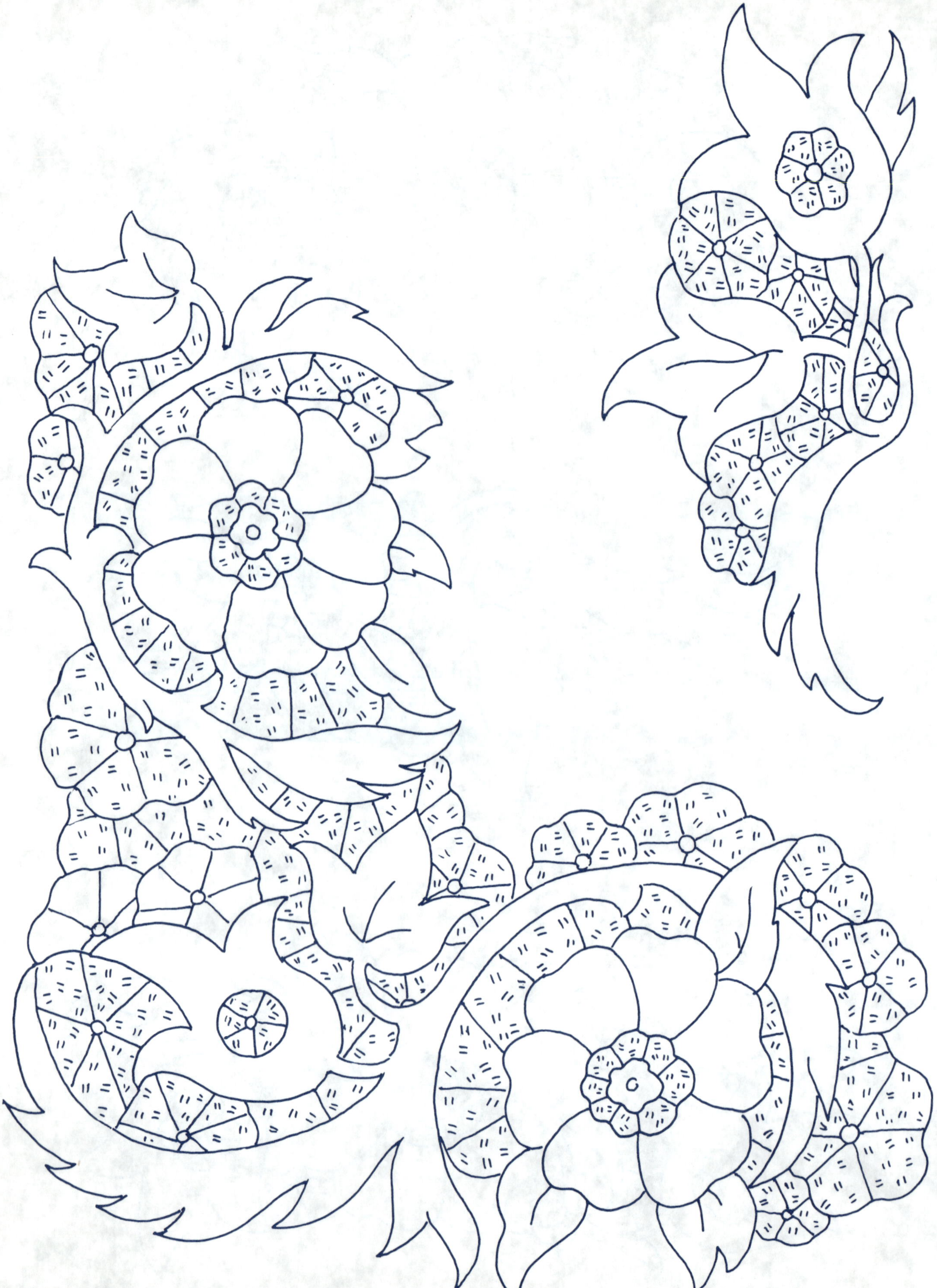

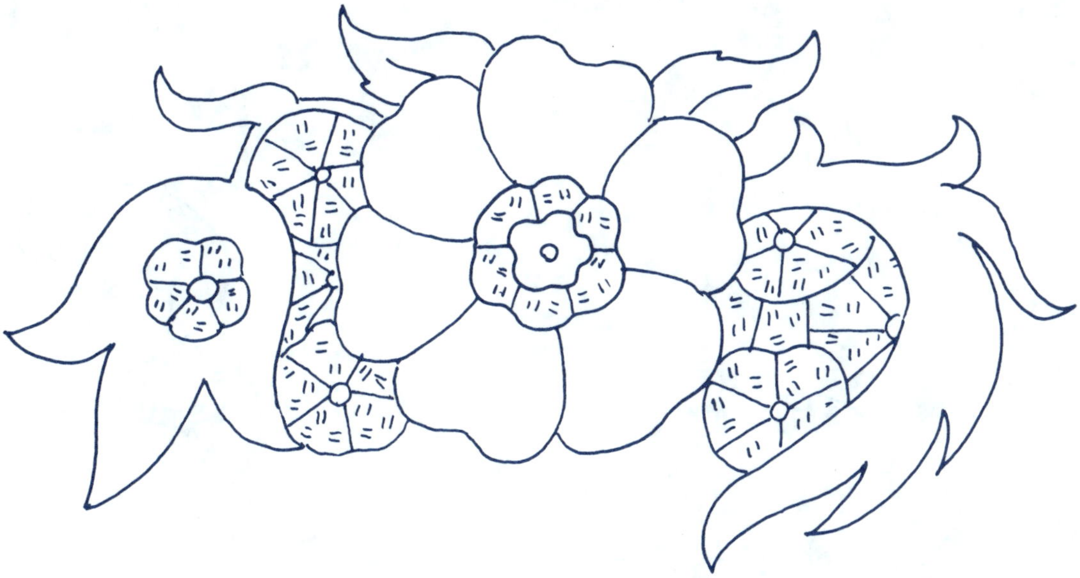

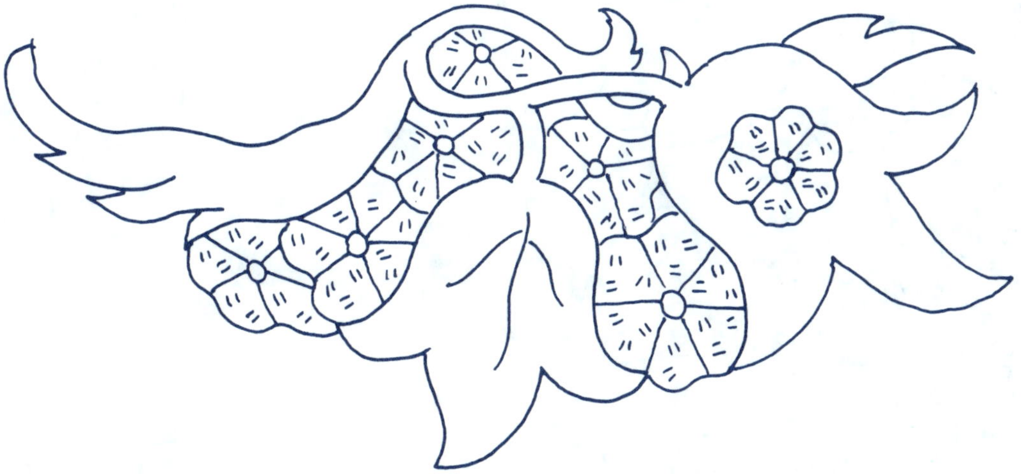

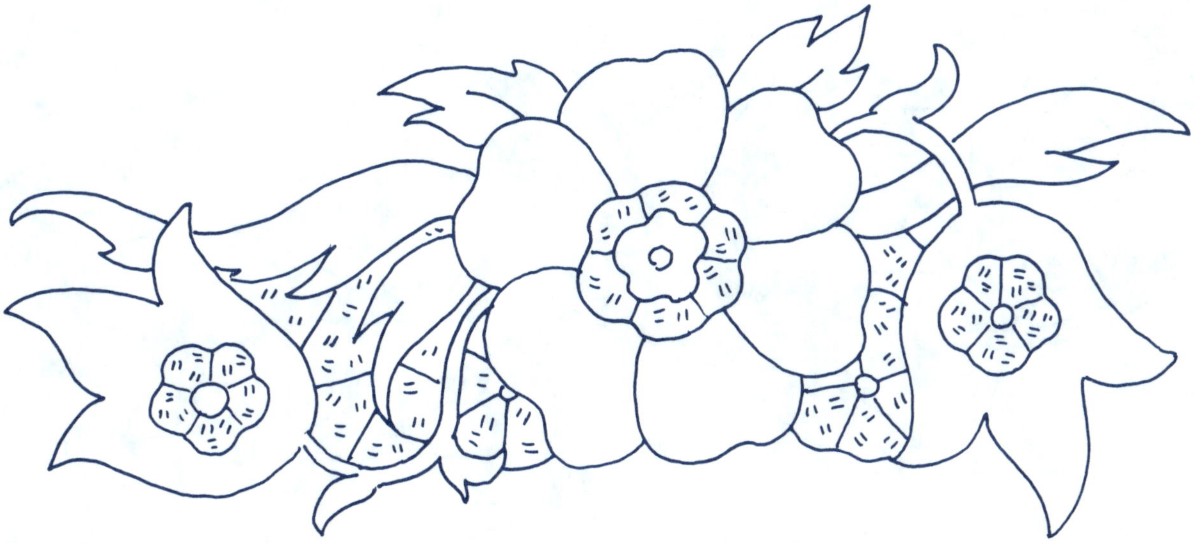

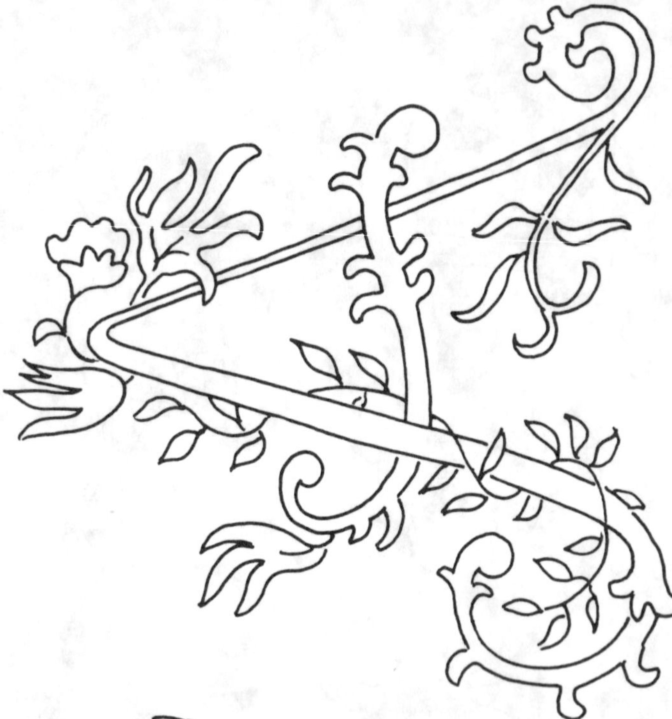

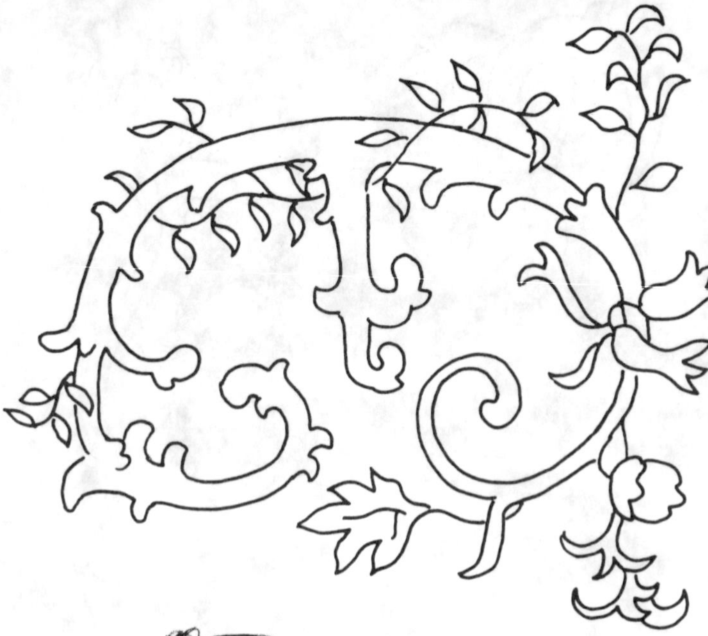

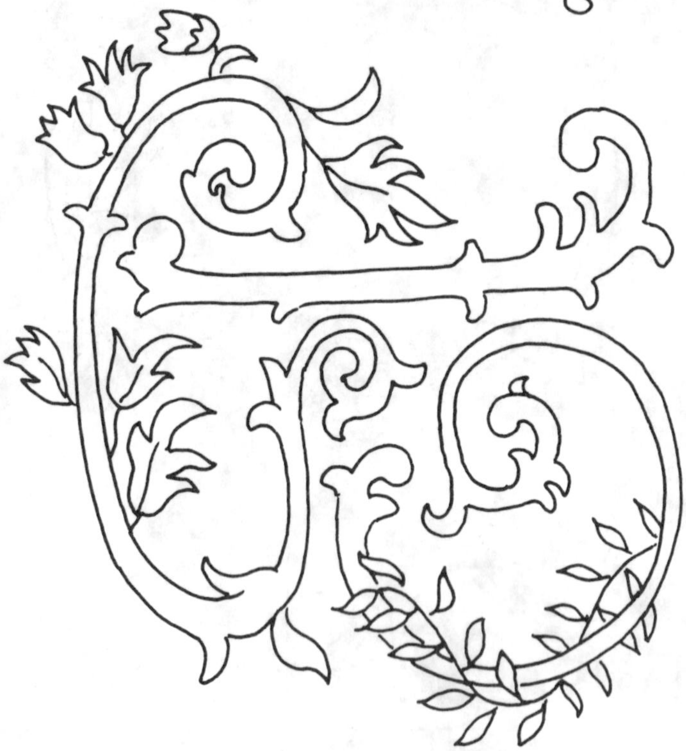

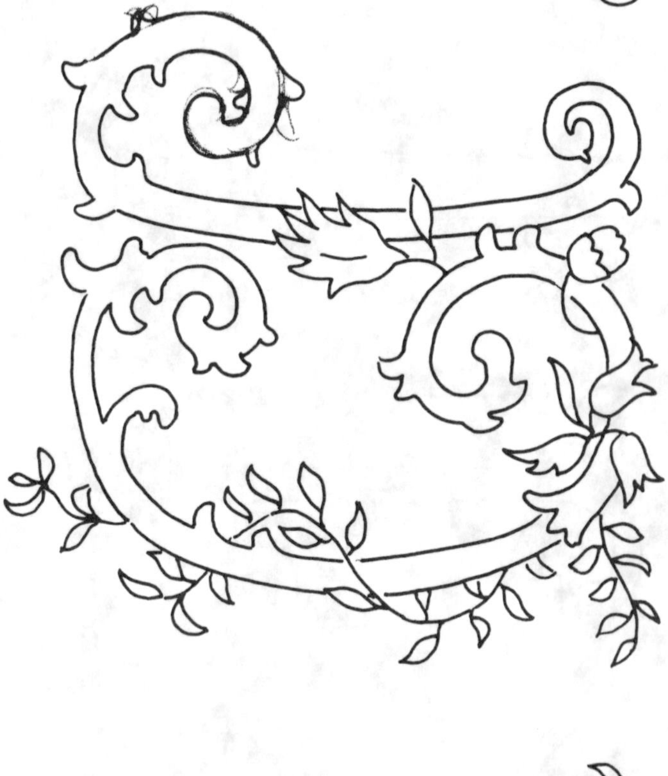

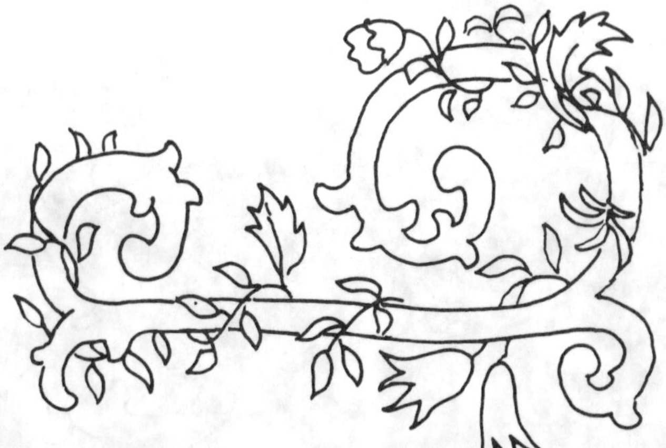

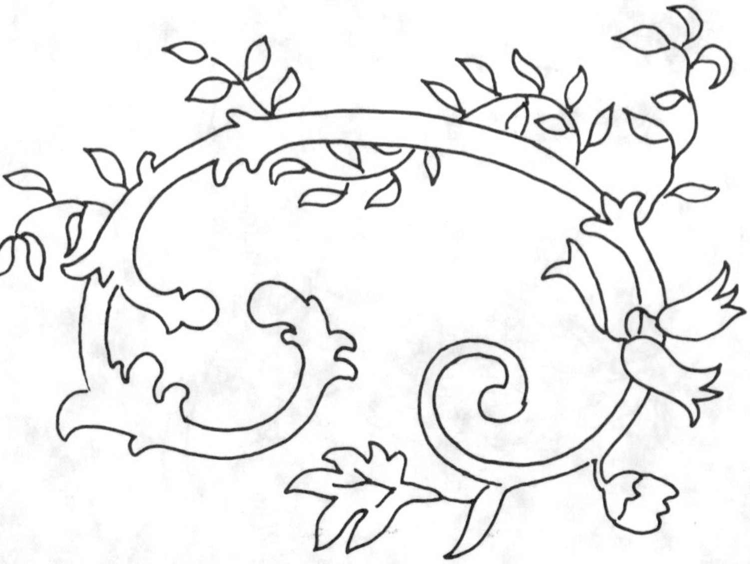

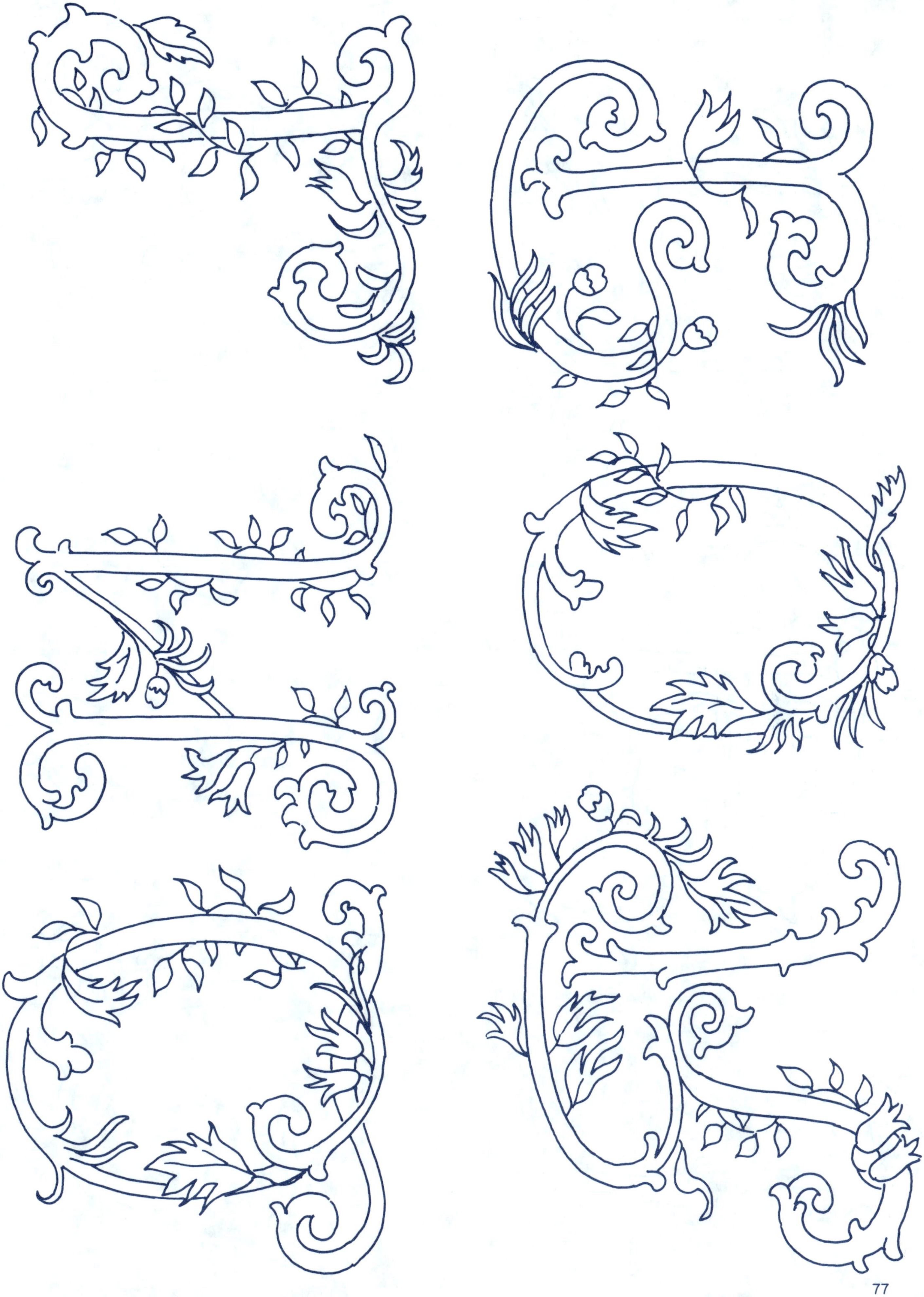

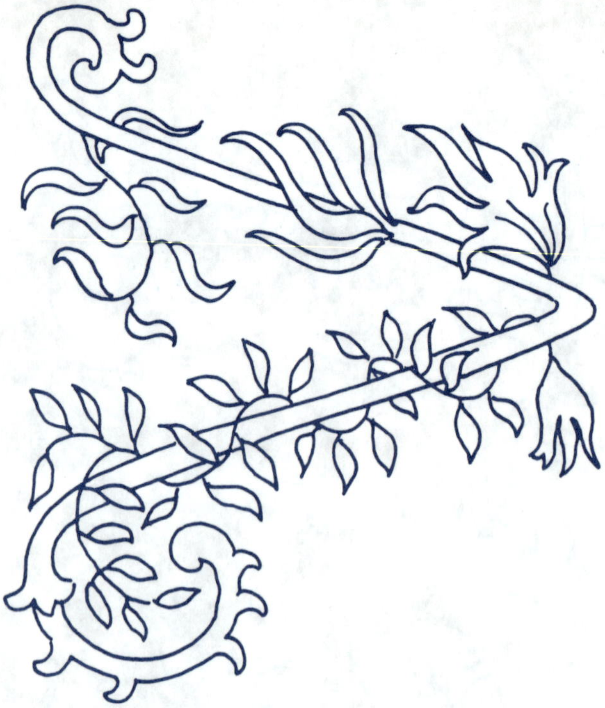
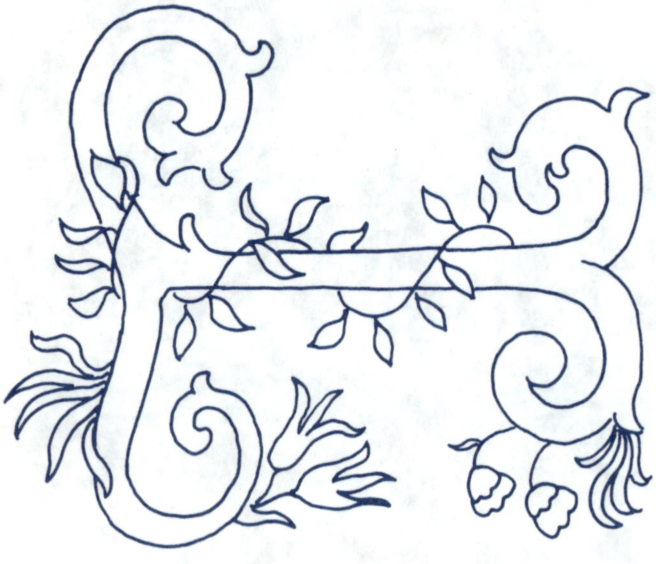
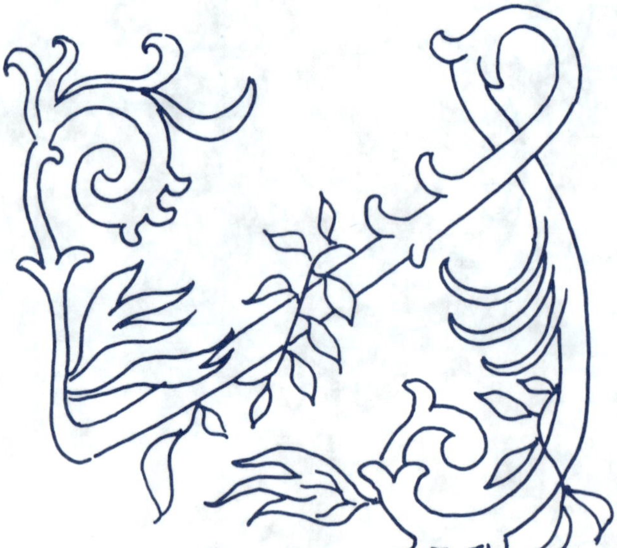
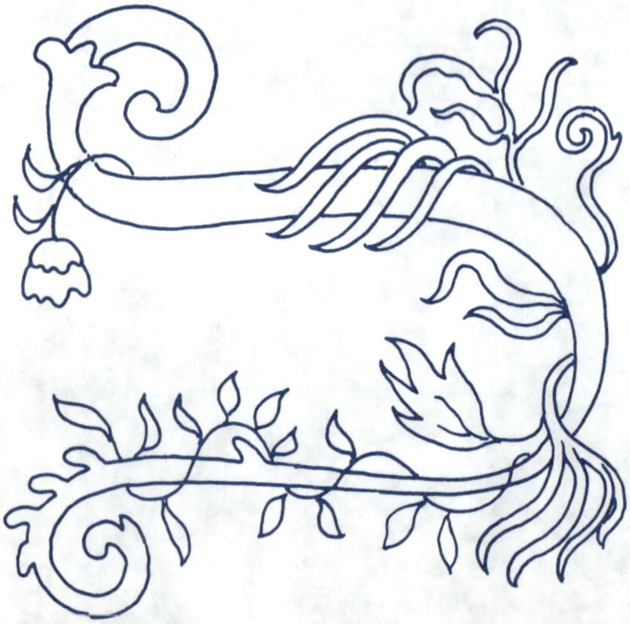
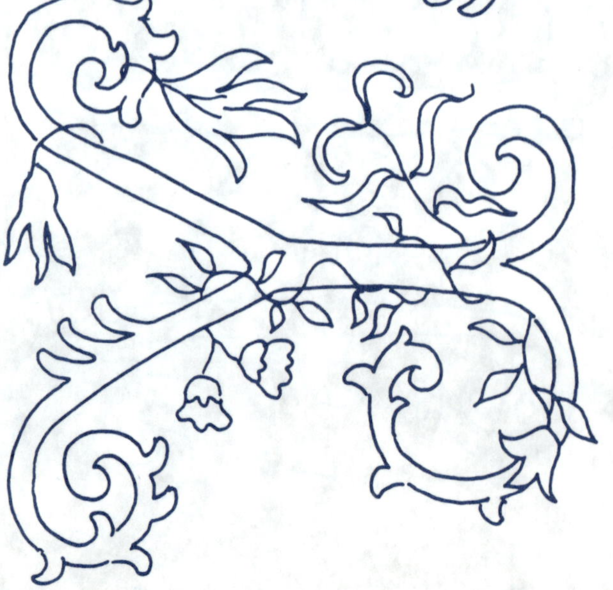

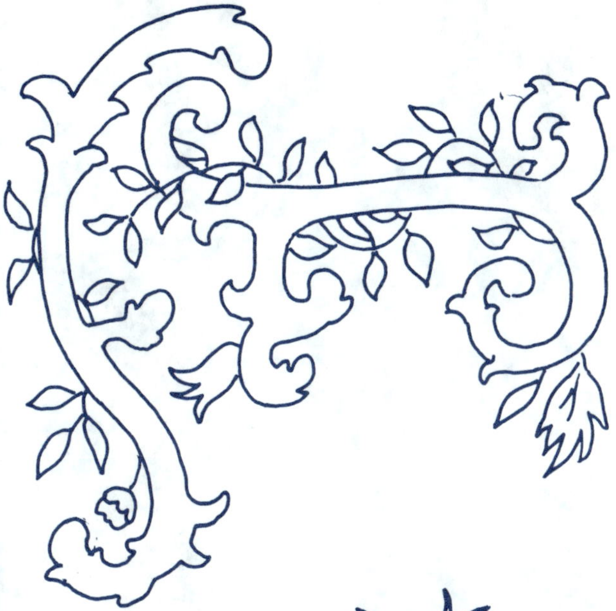

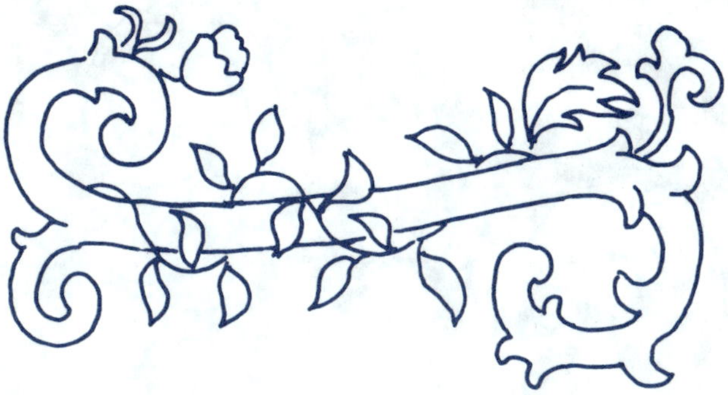

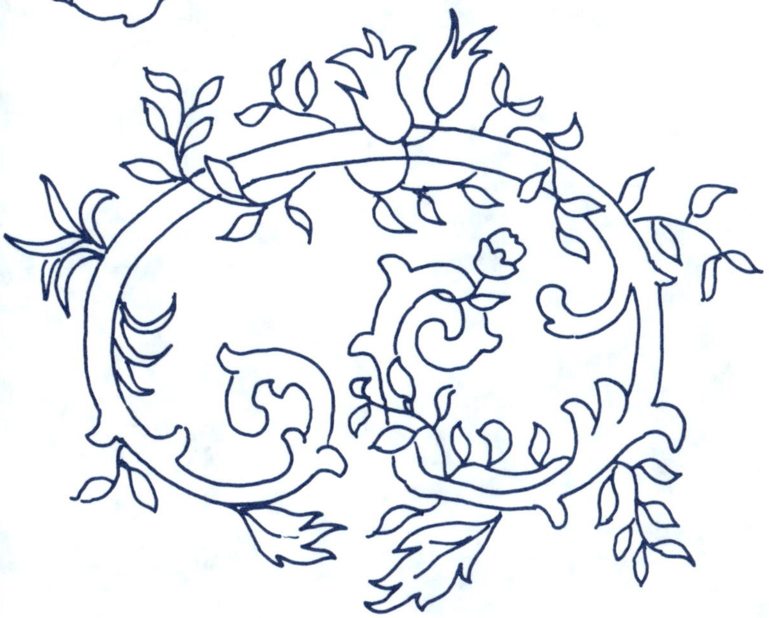

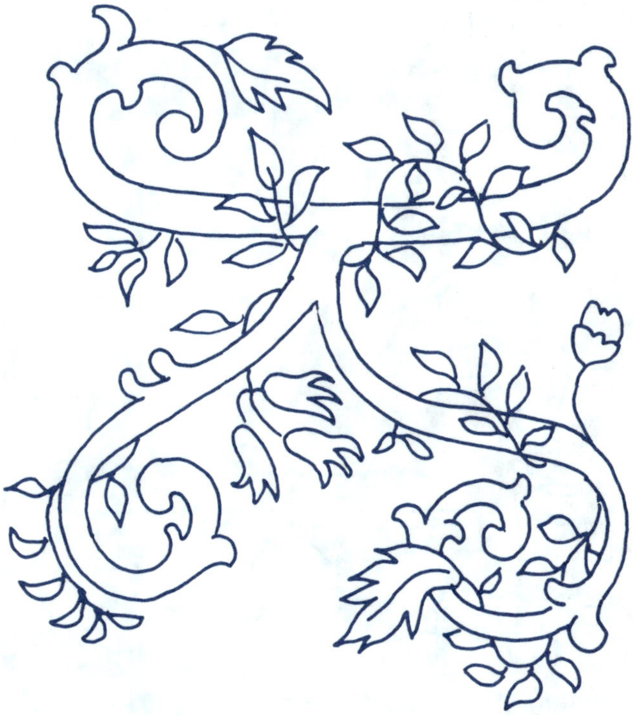

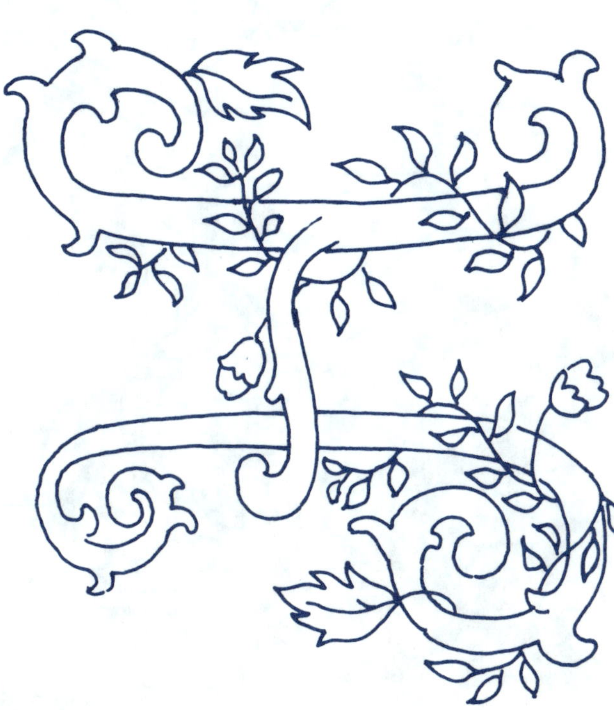

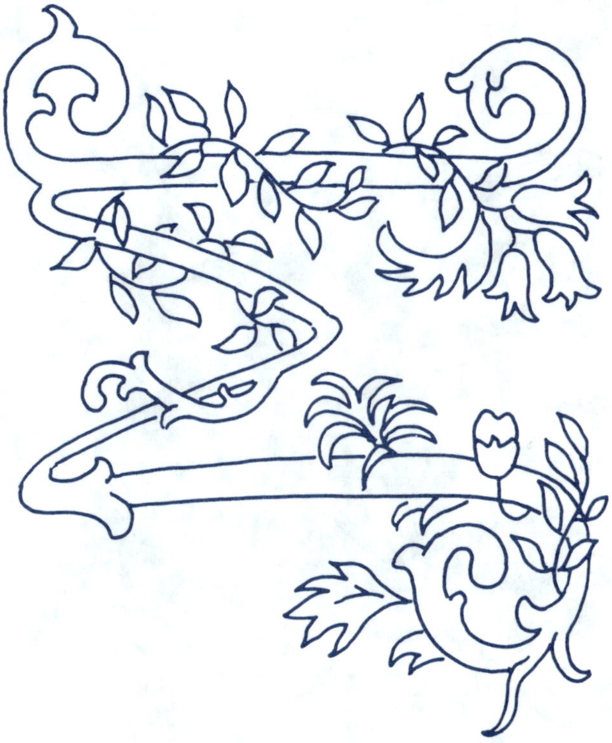

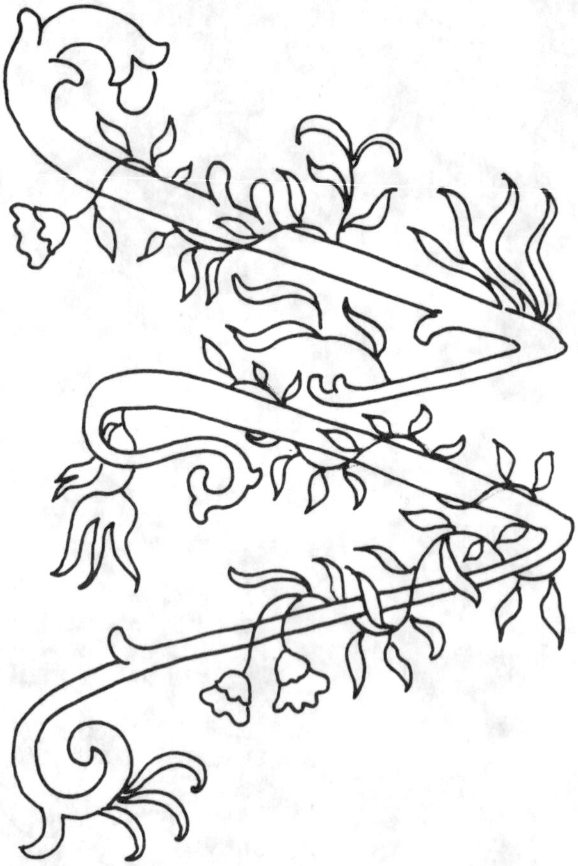

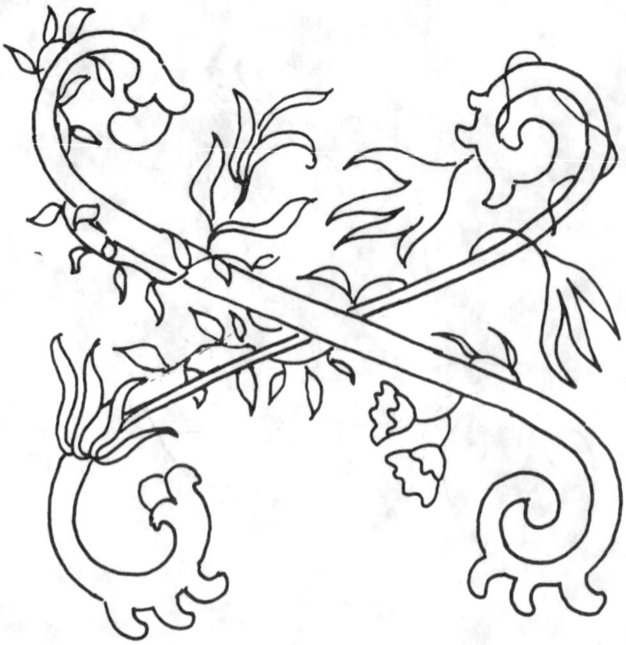

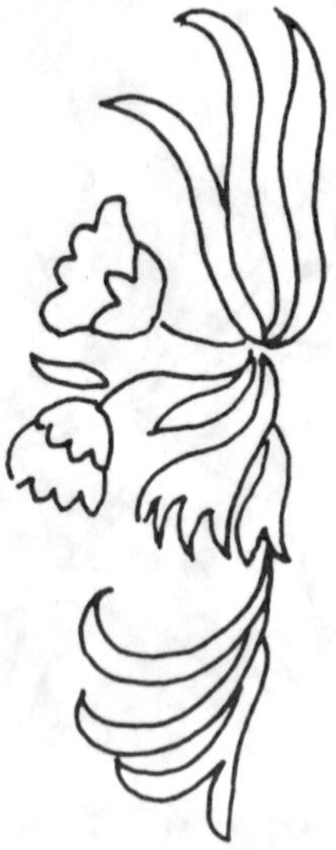

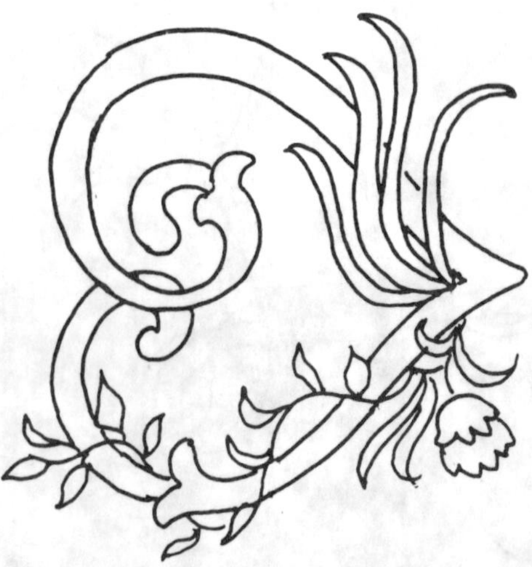

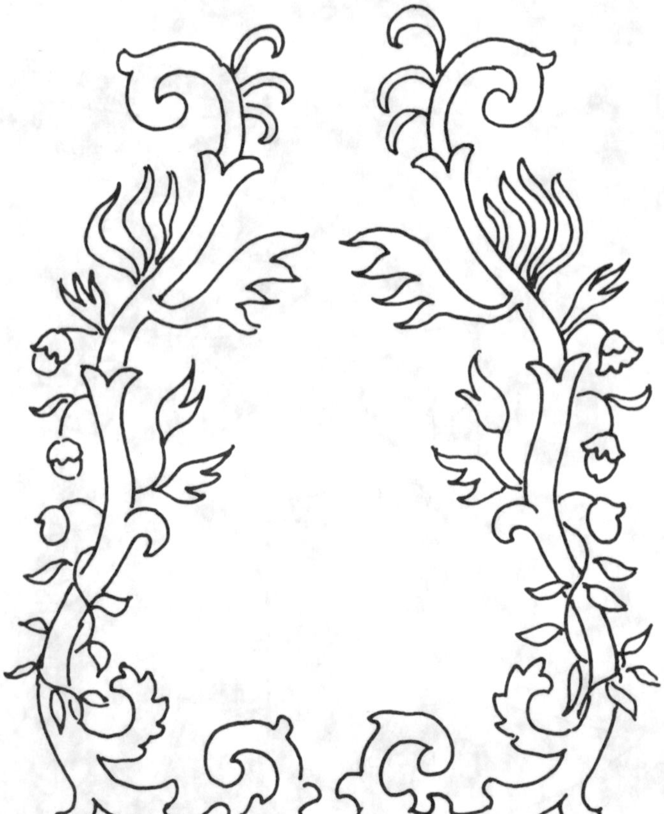

85

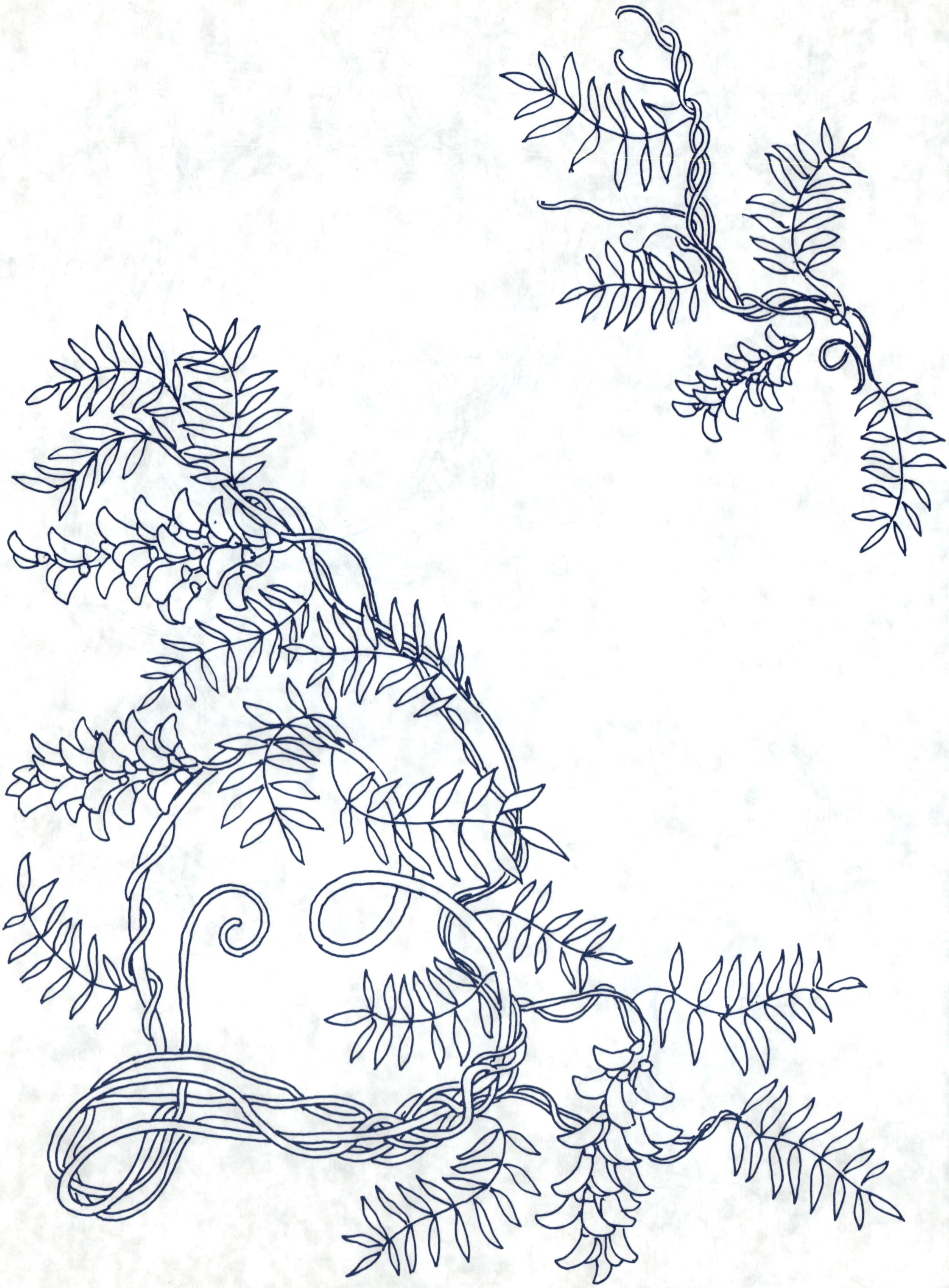

89

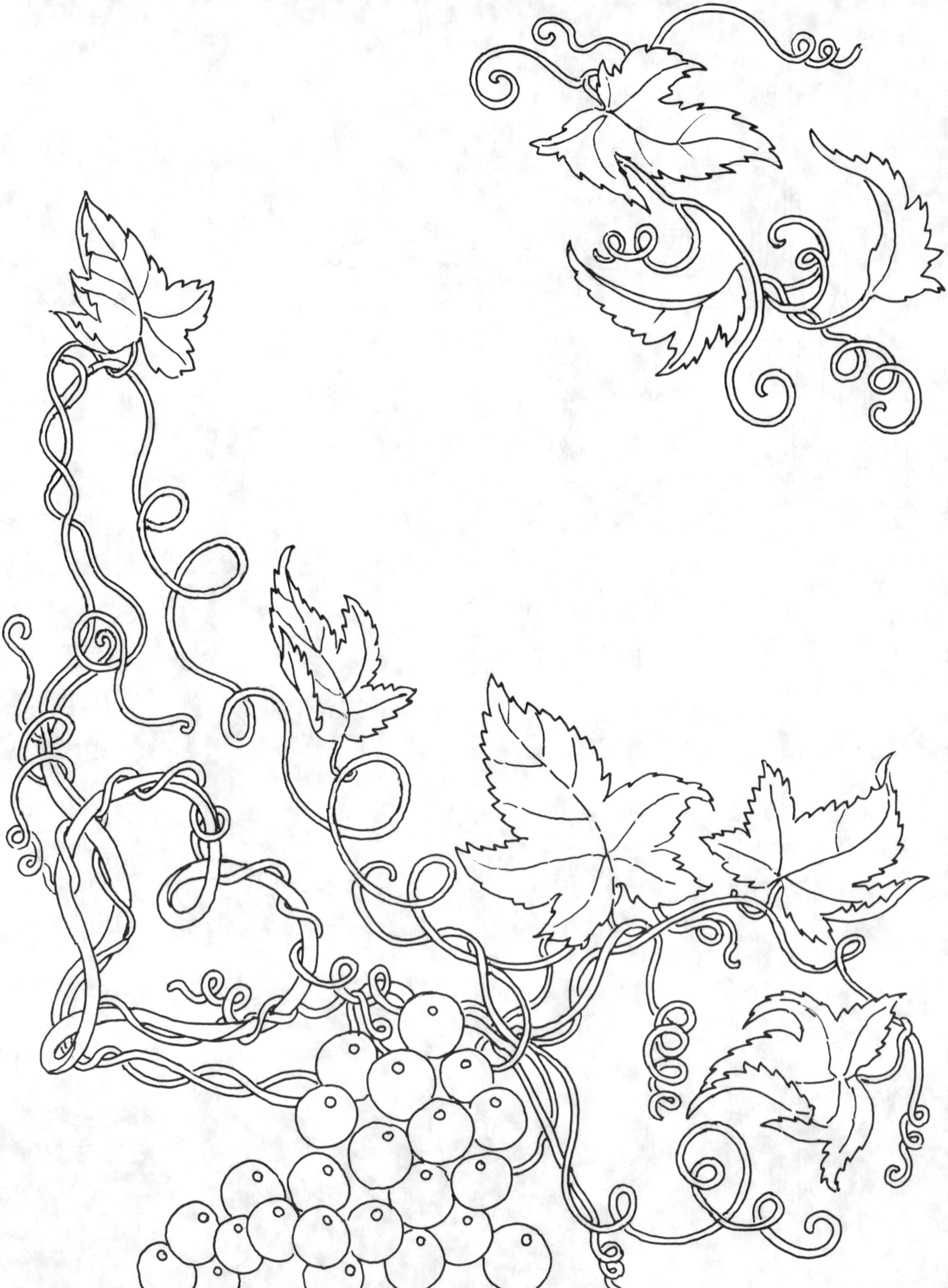

93

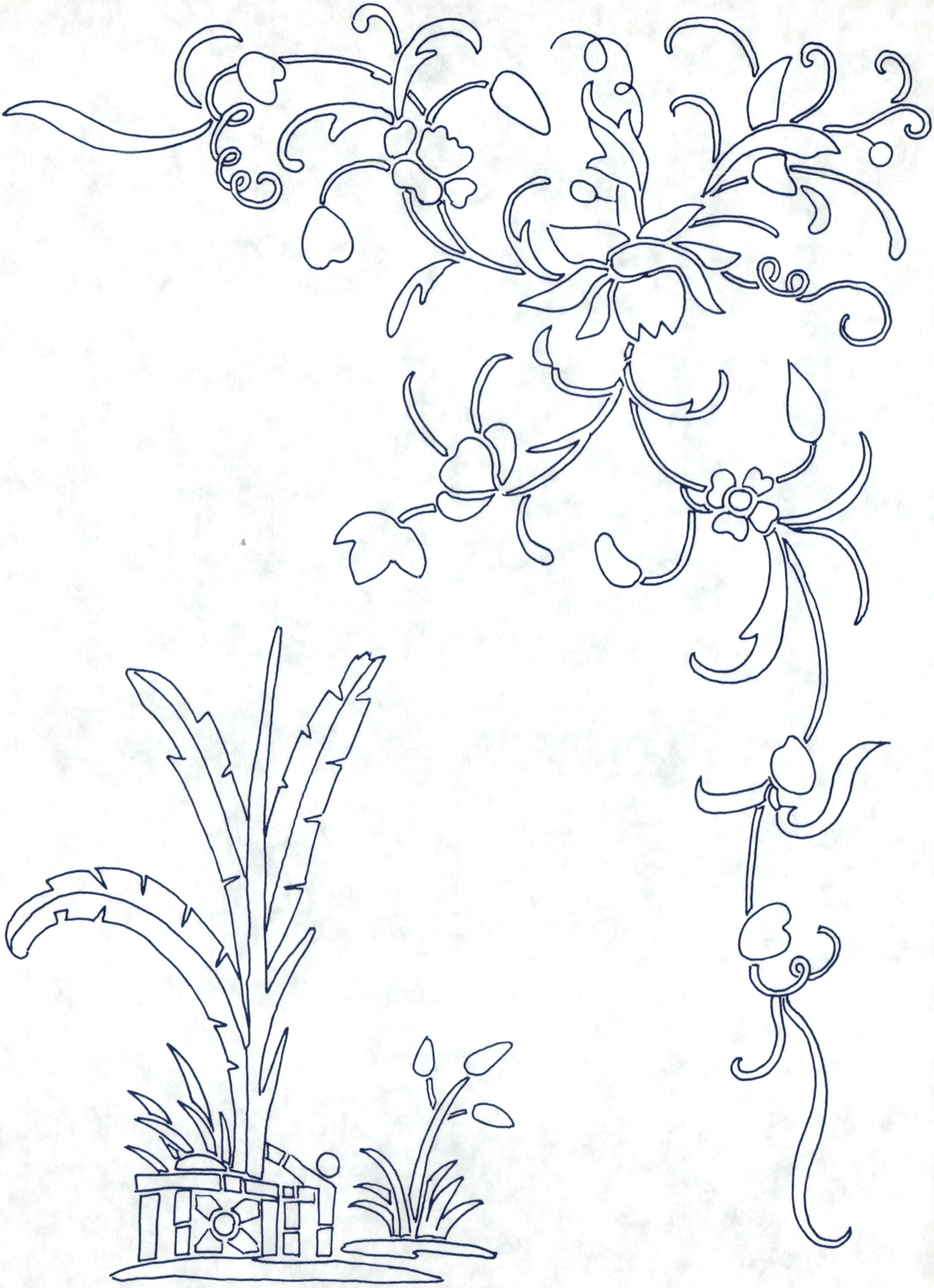

97

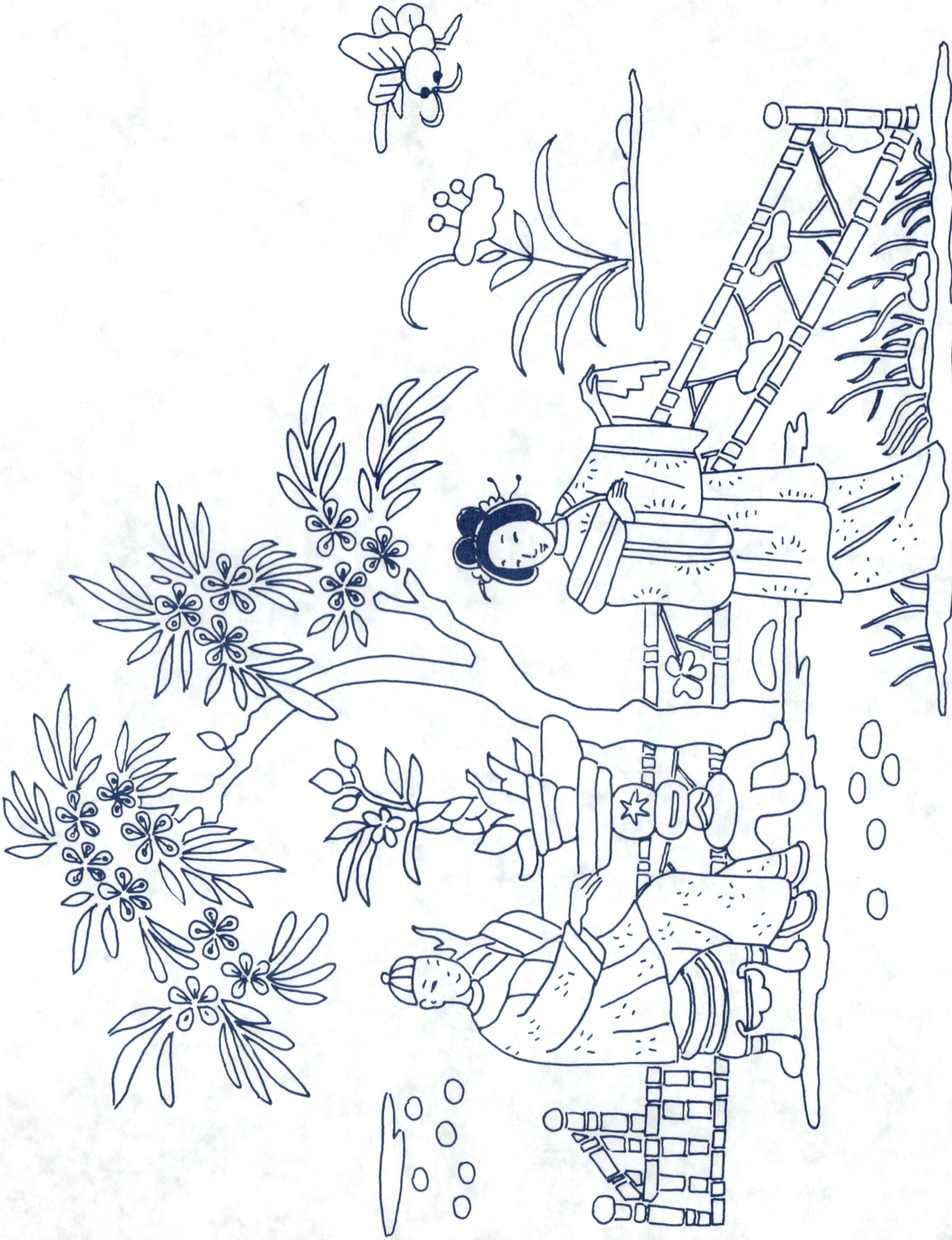

101

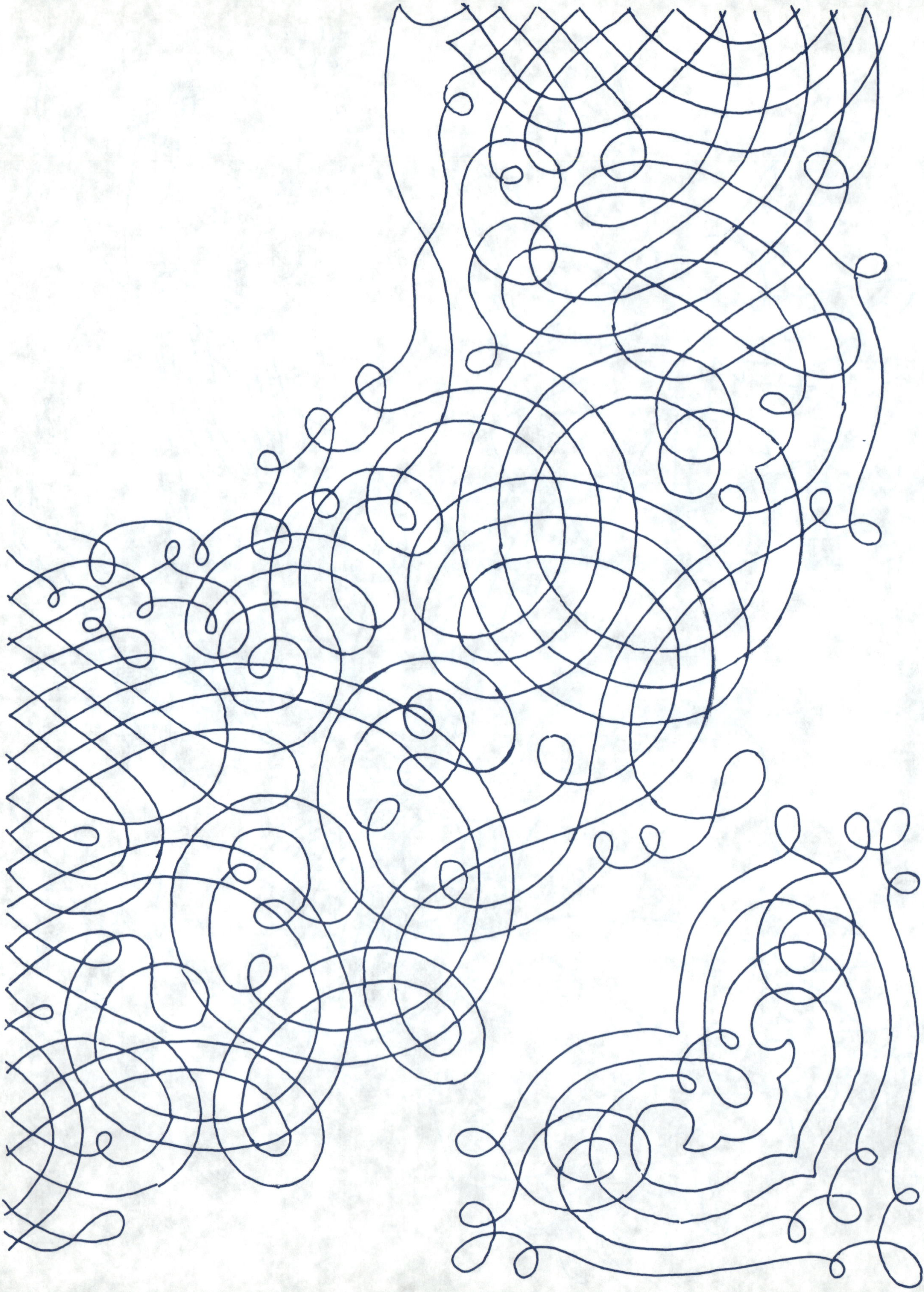

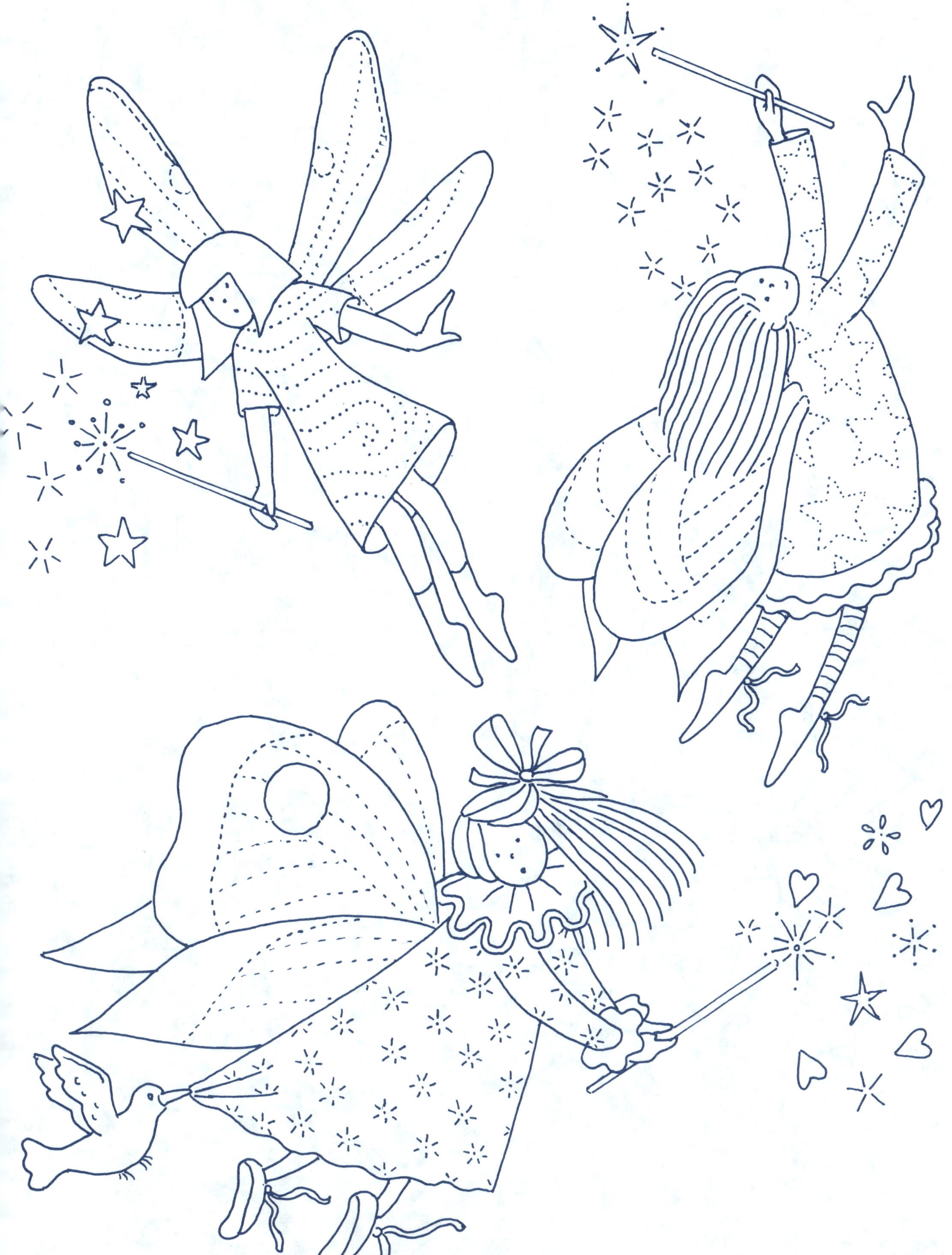

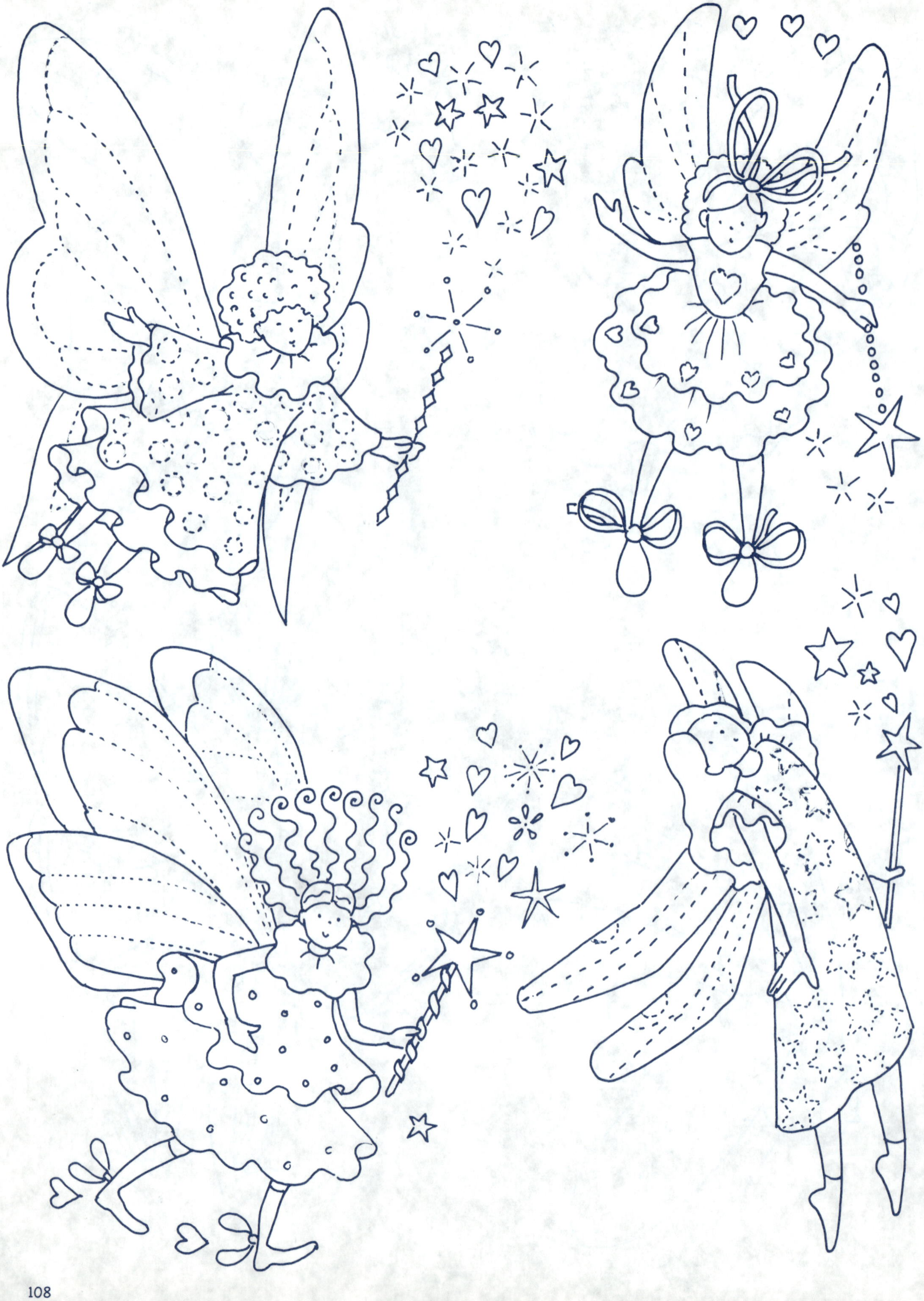

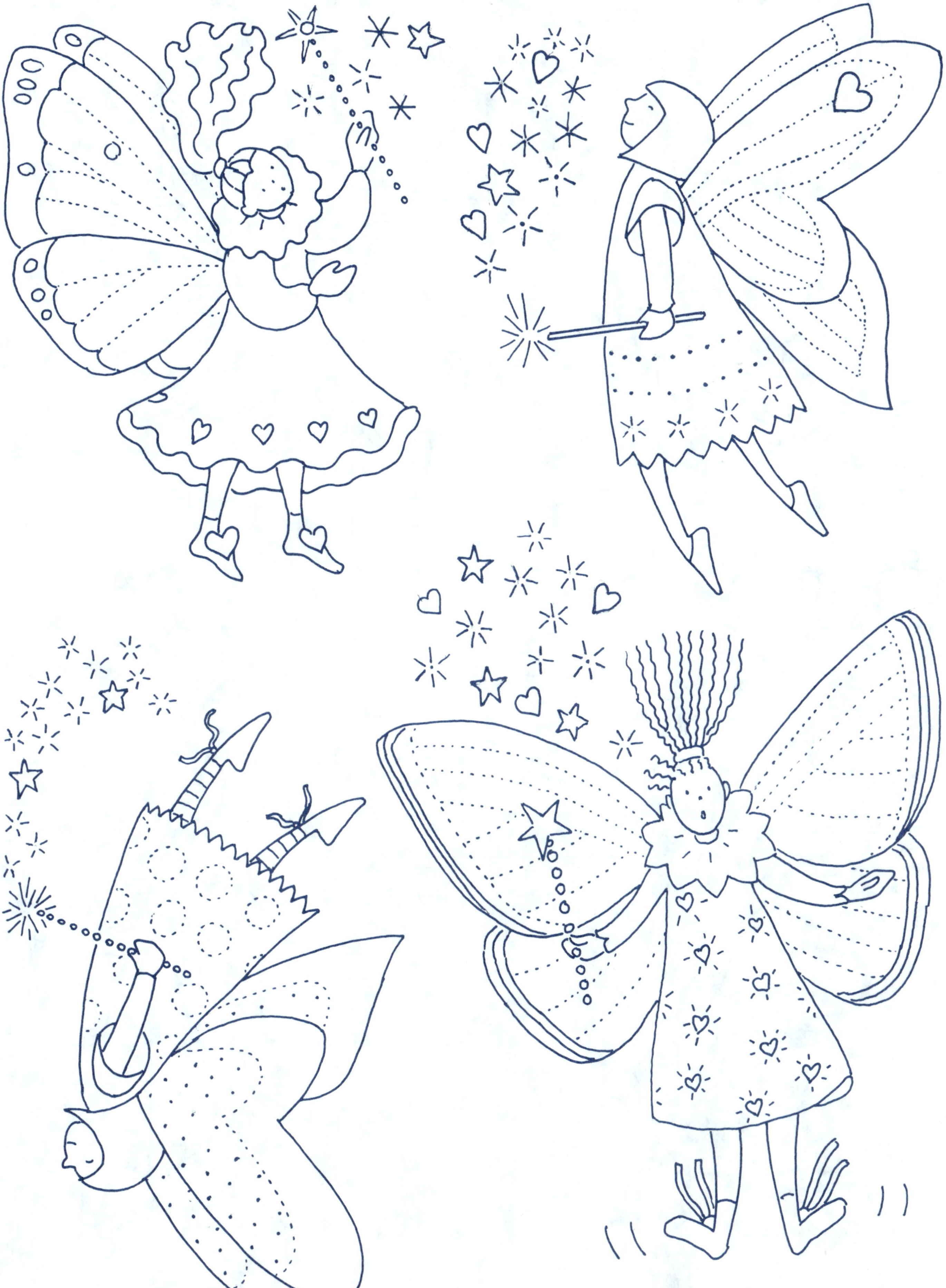

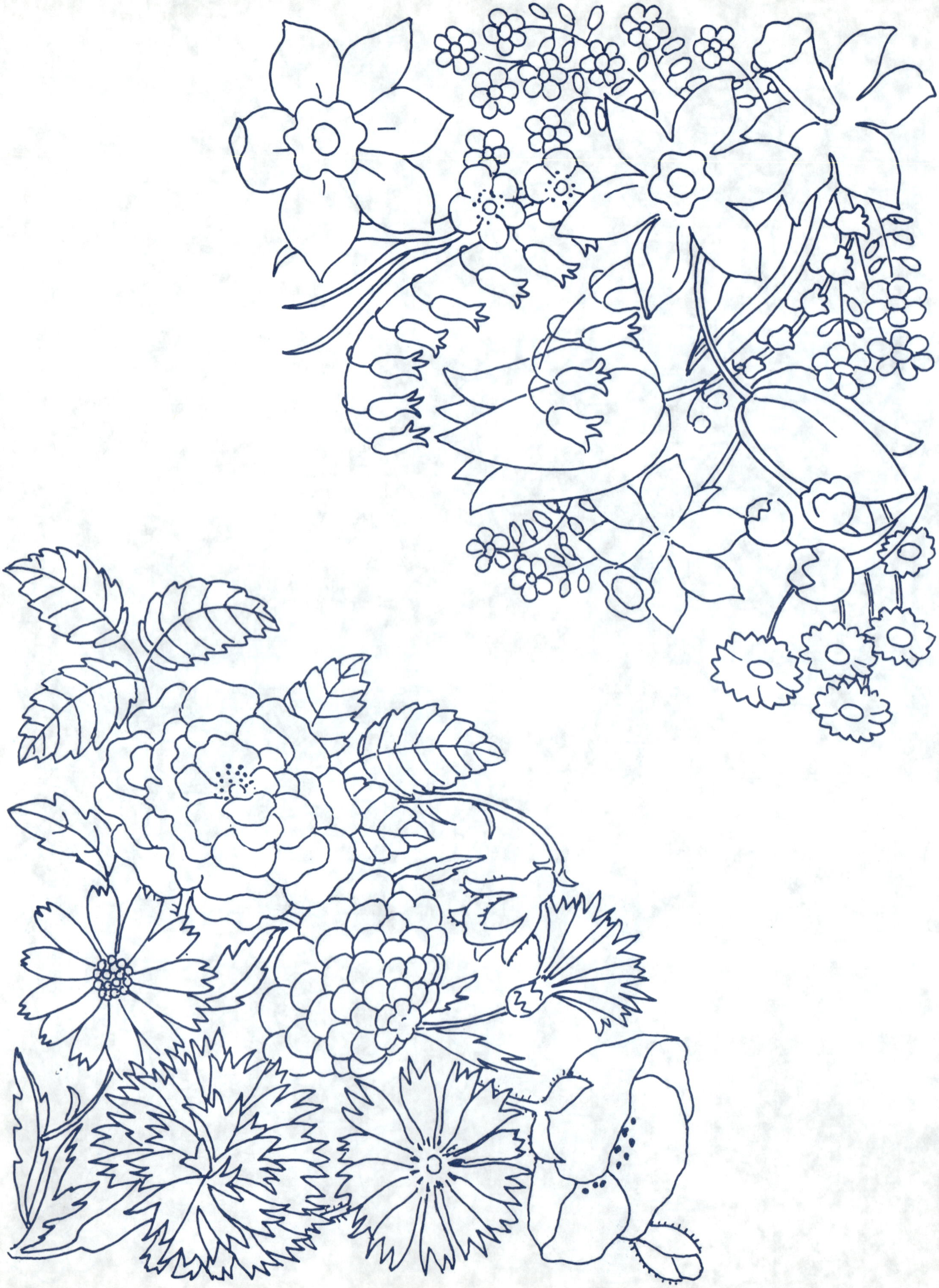

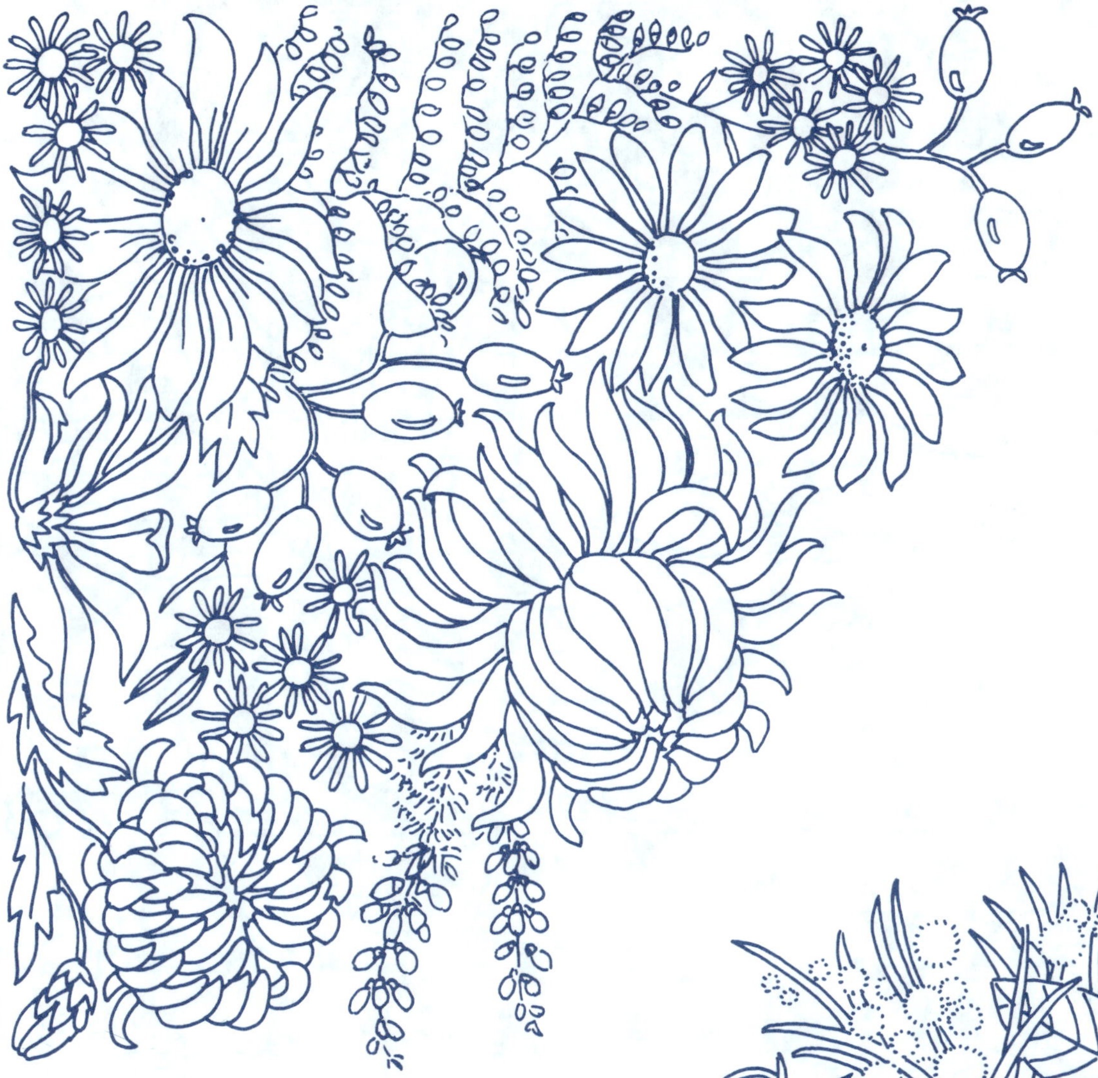

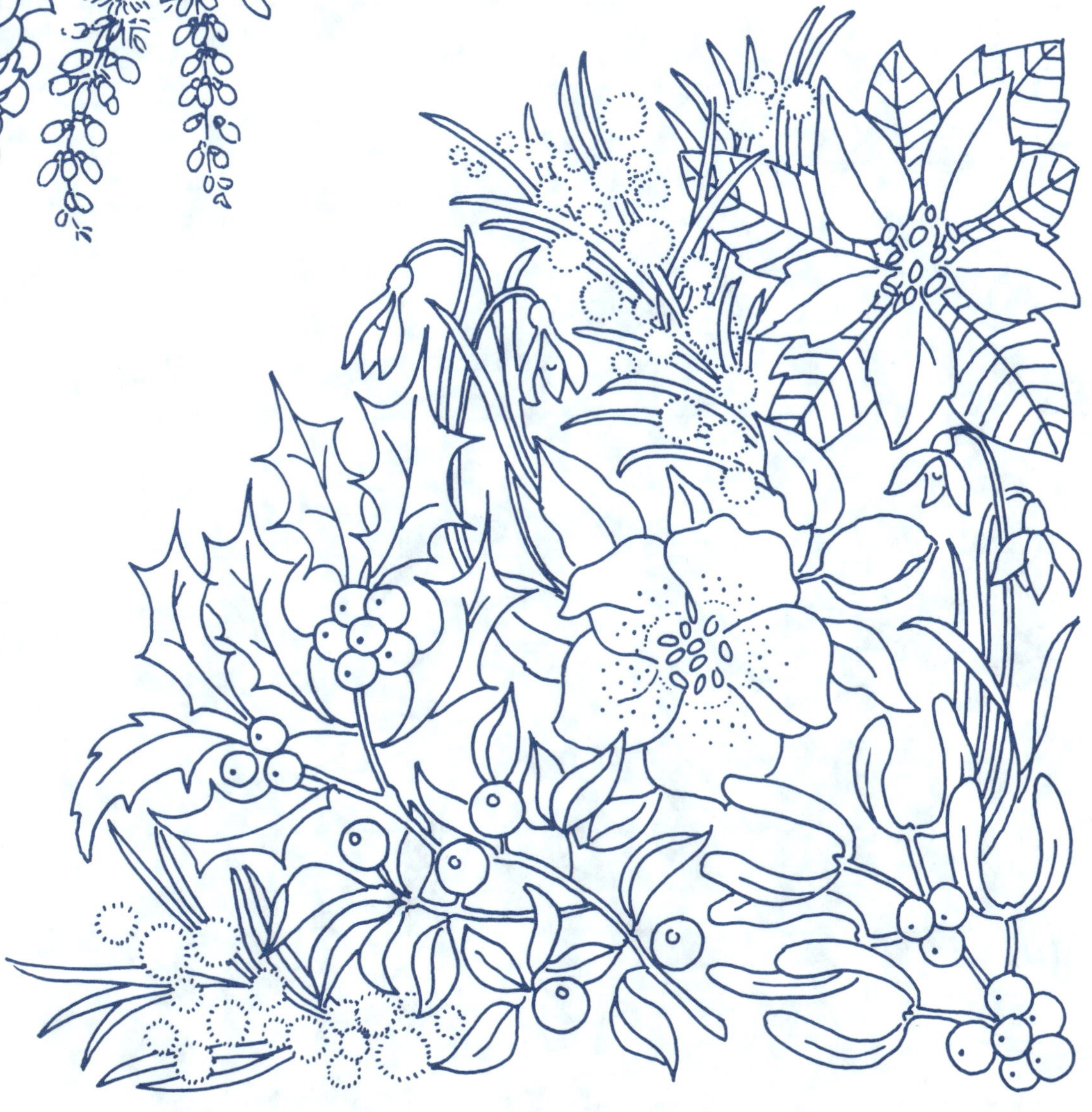

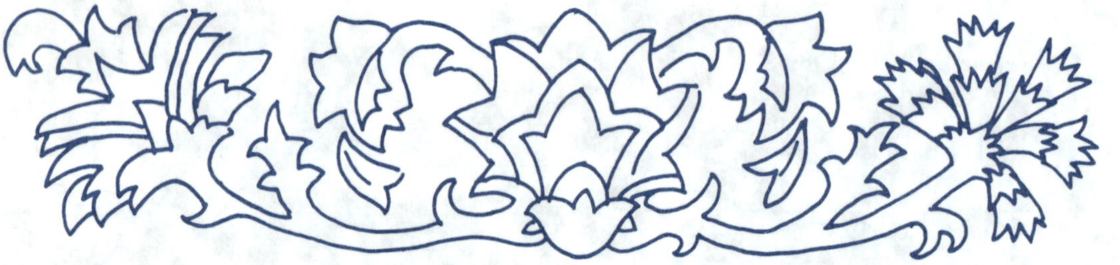

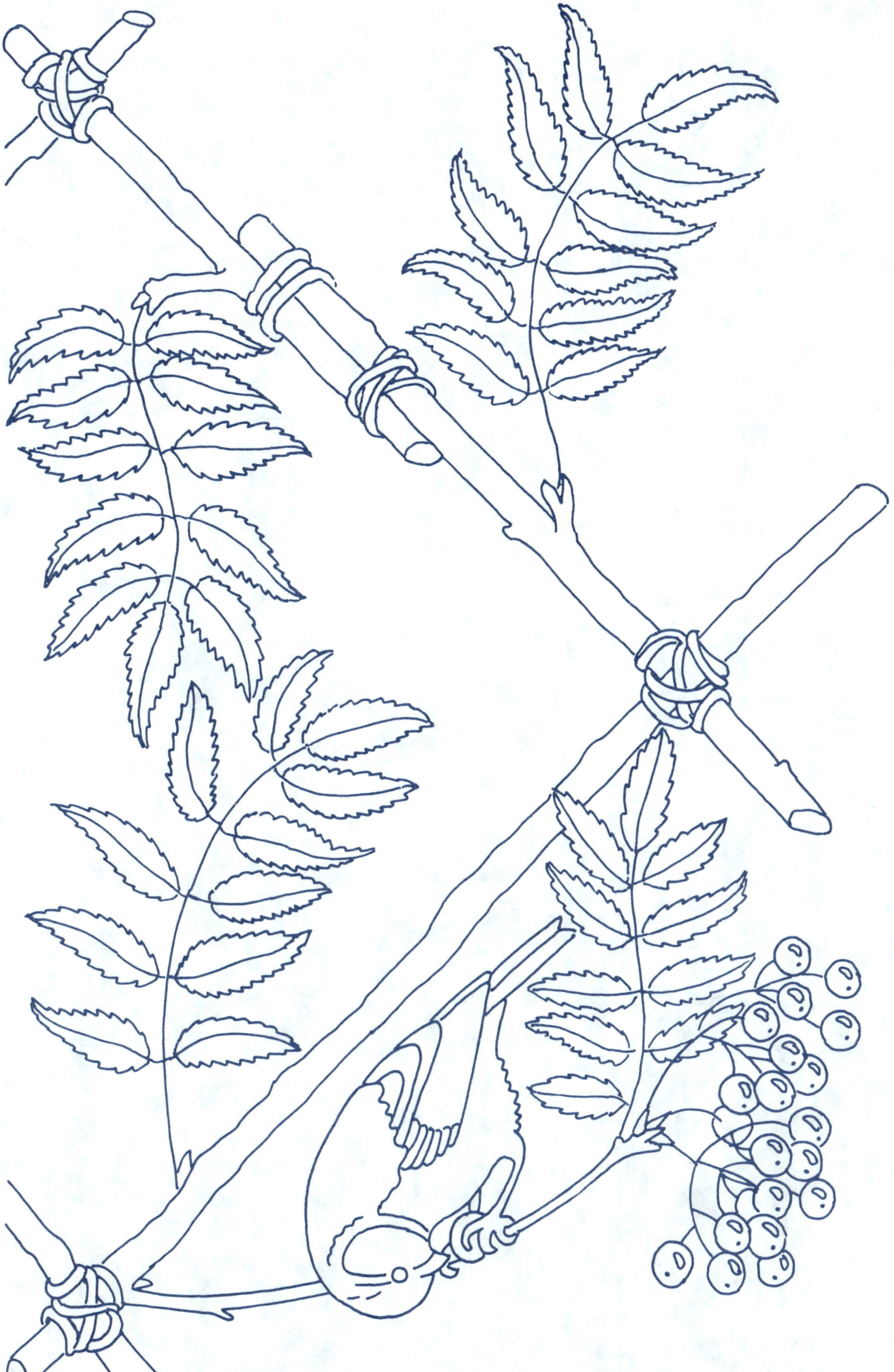

120

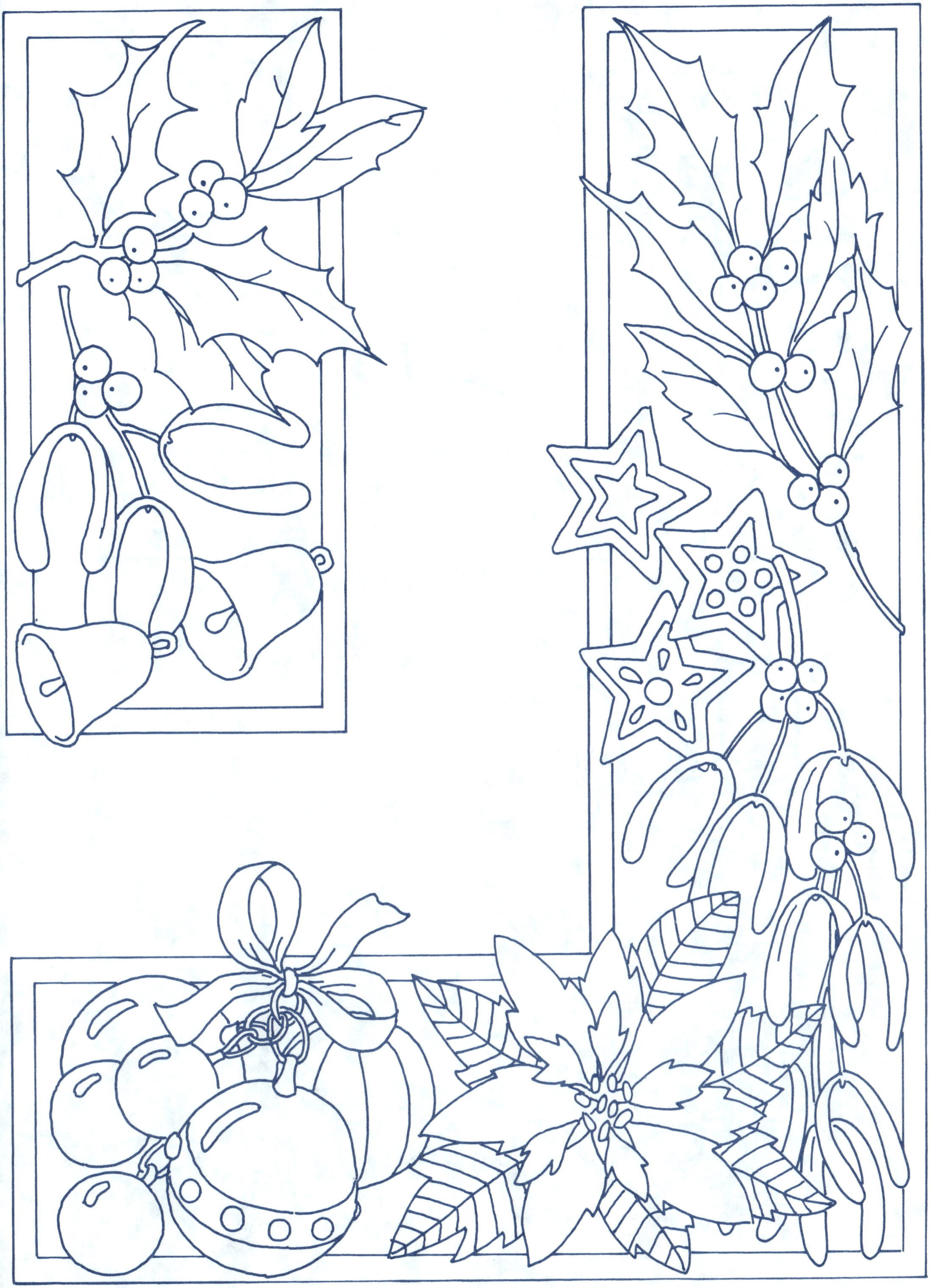

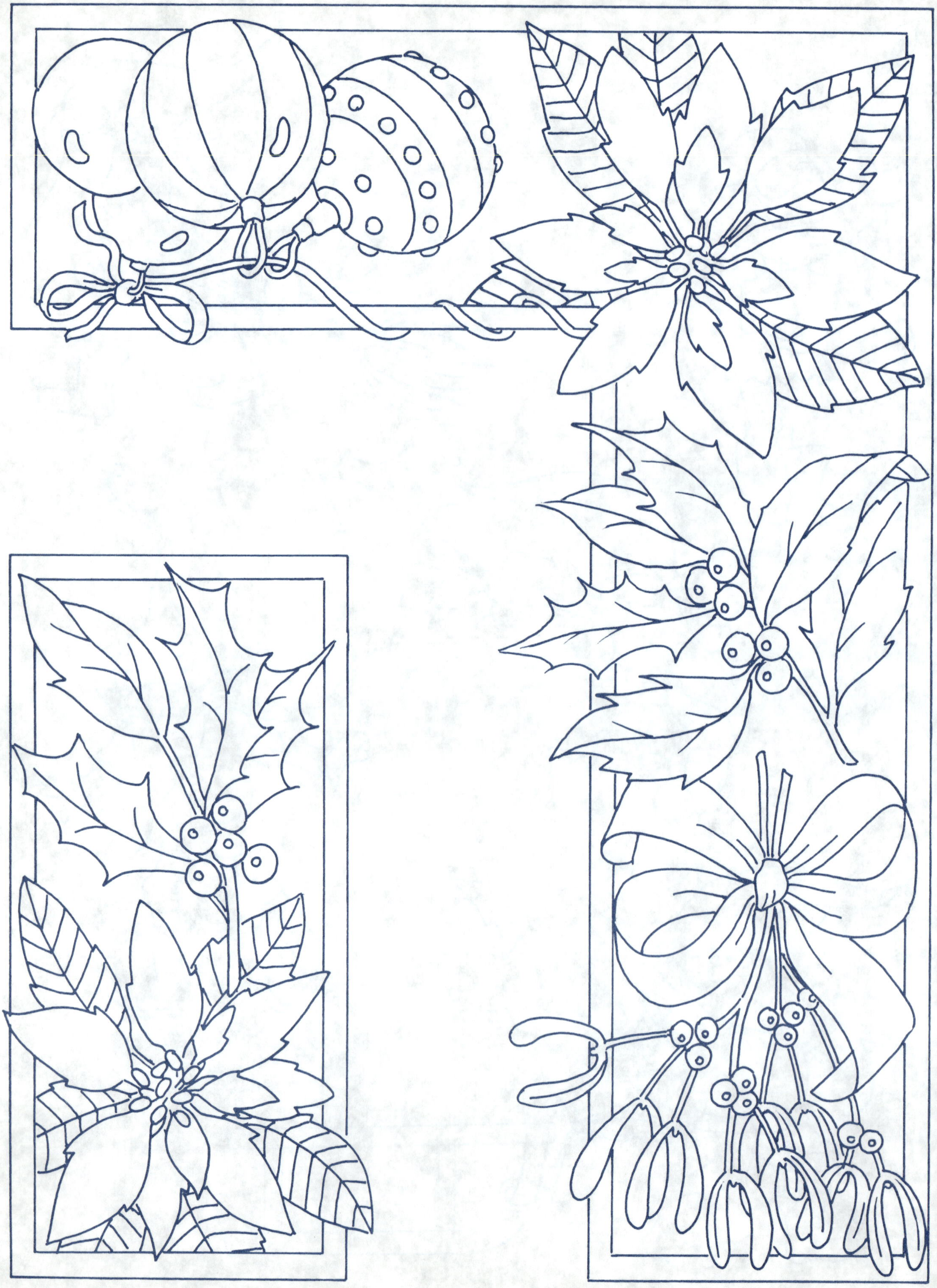

125

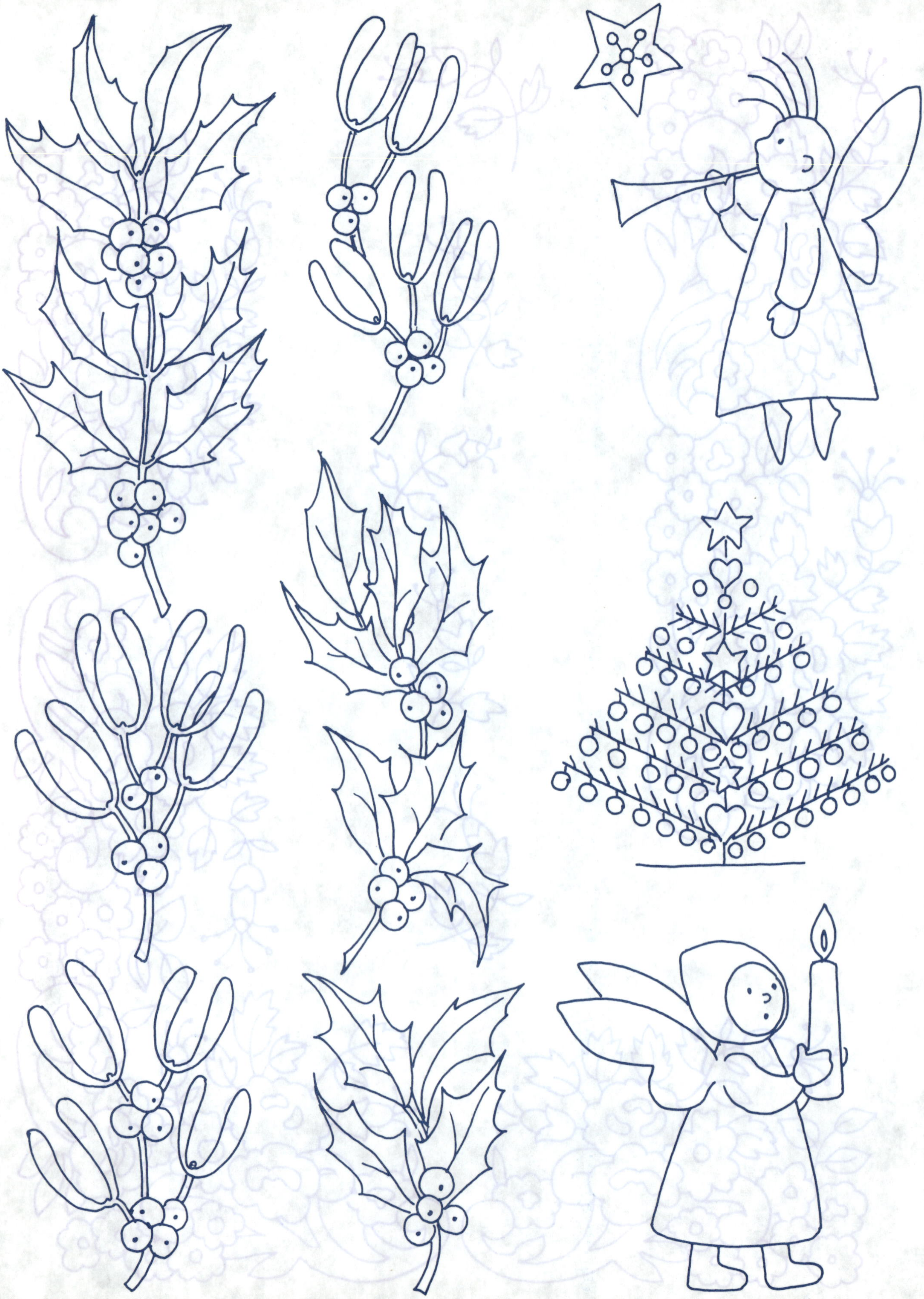

129

132

133

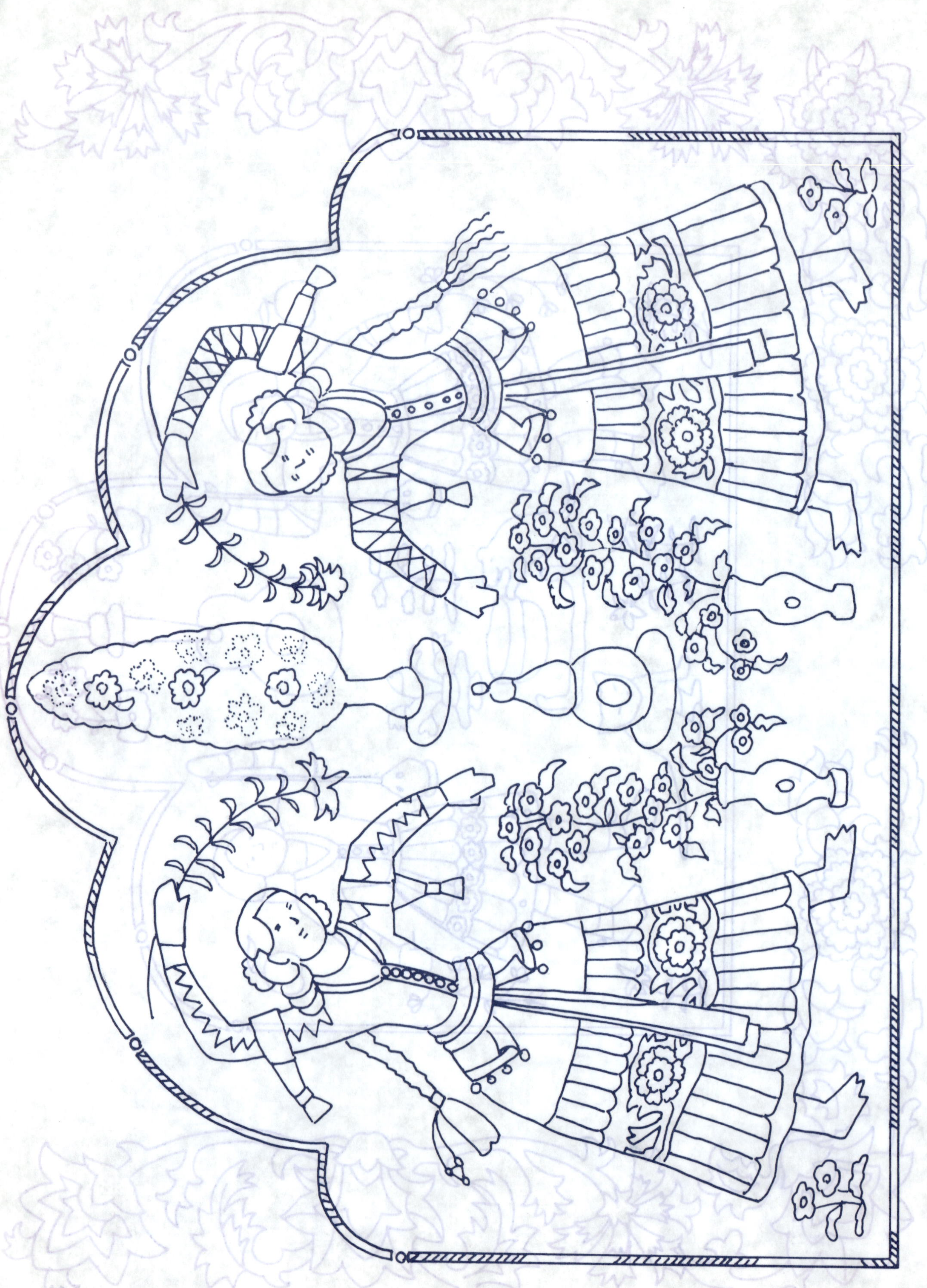

137

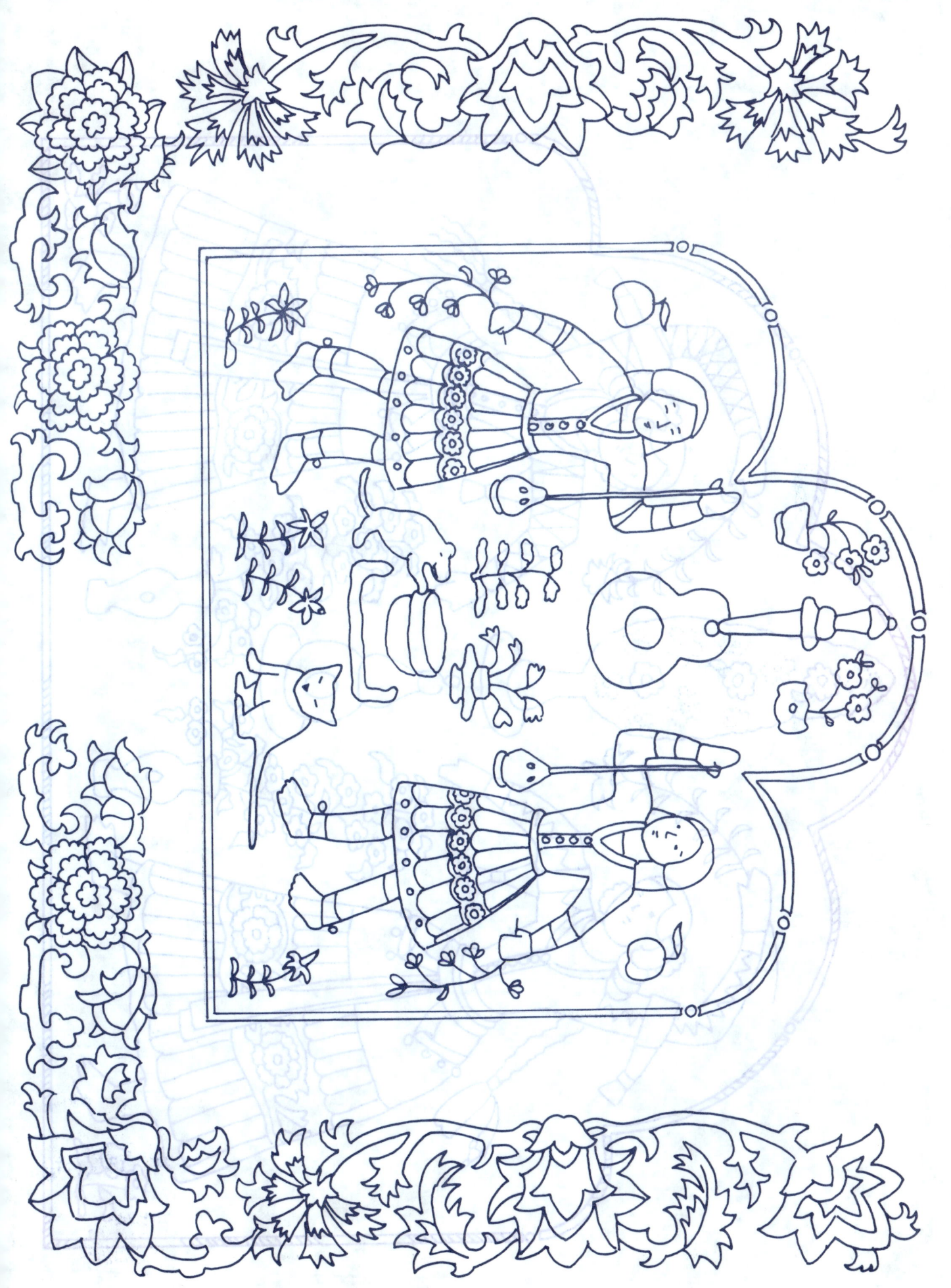

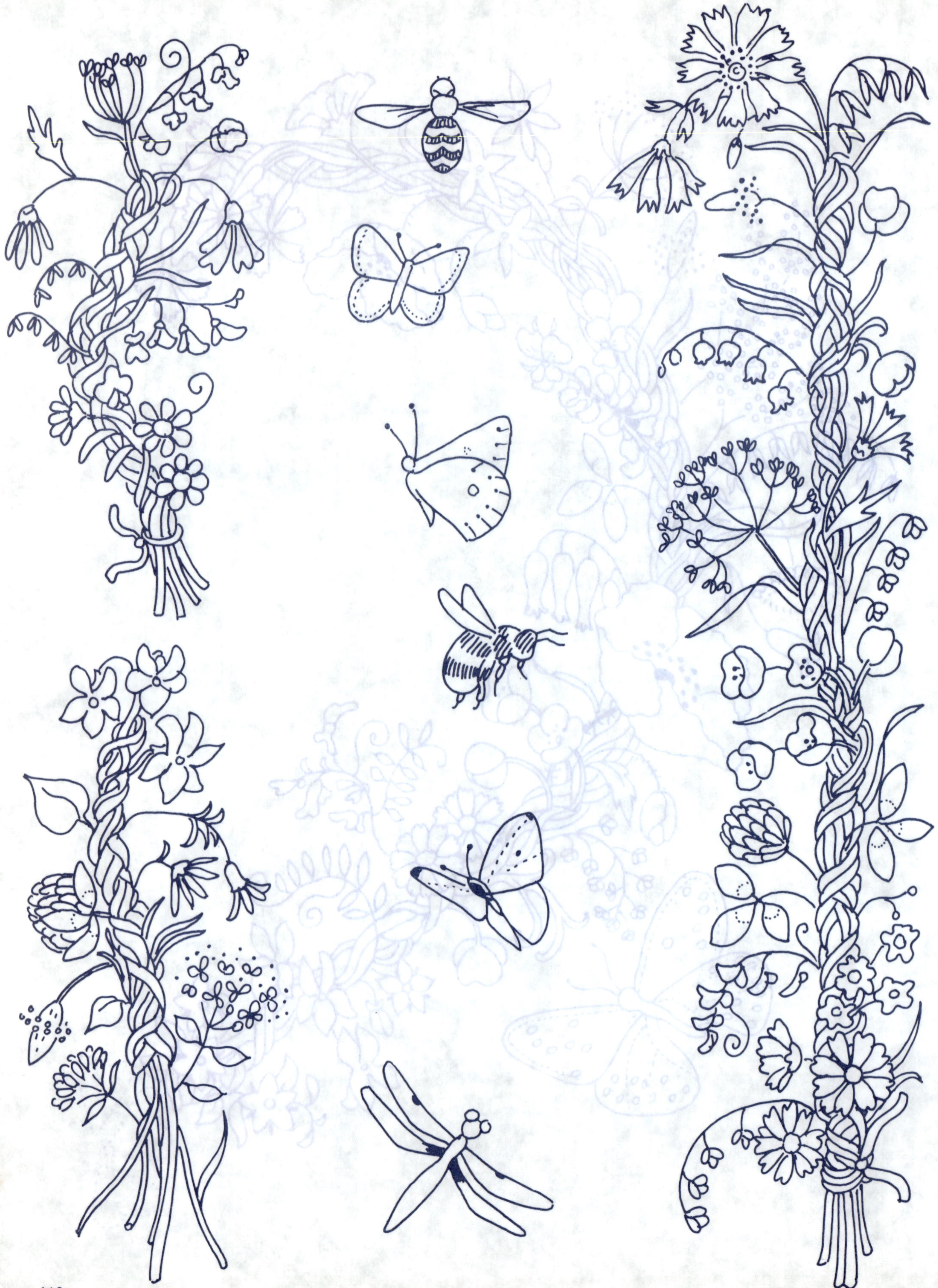

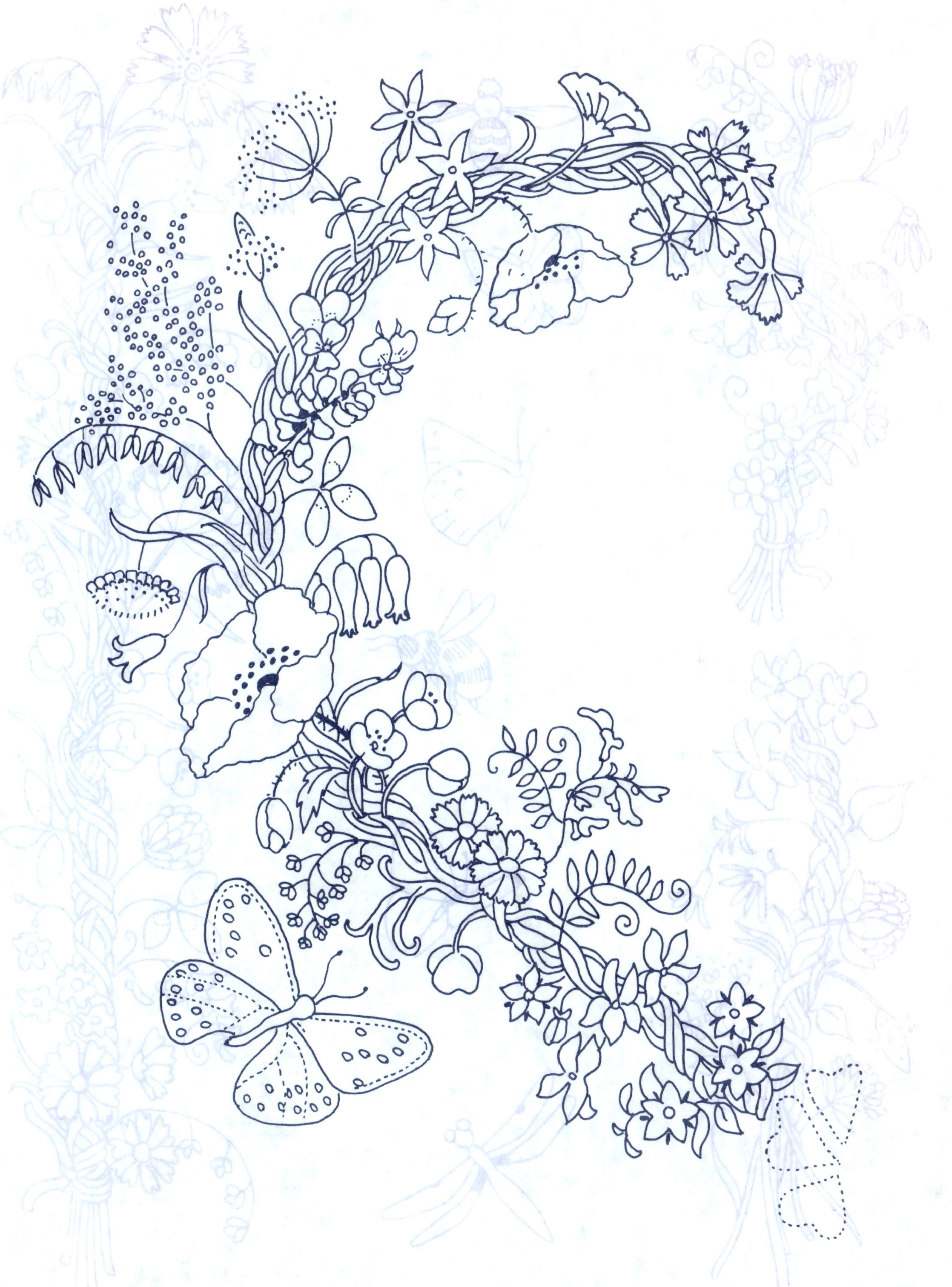

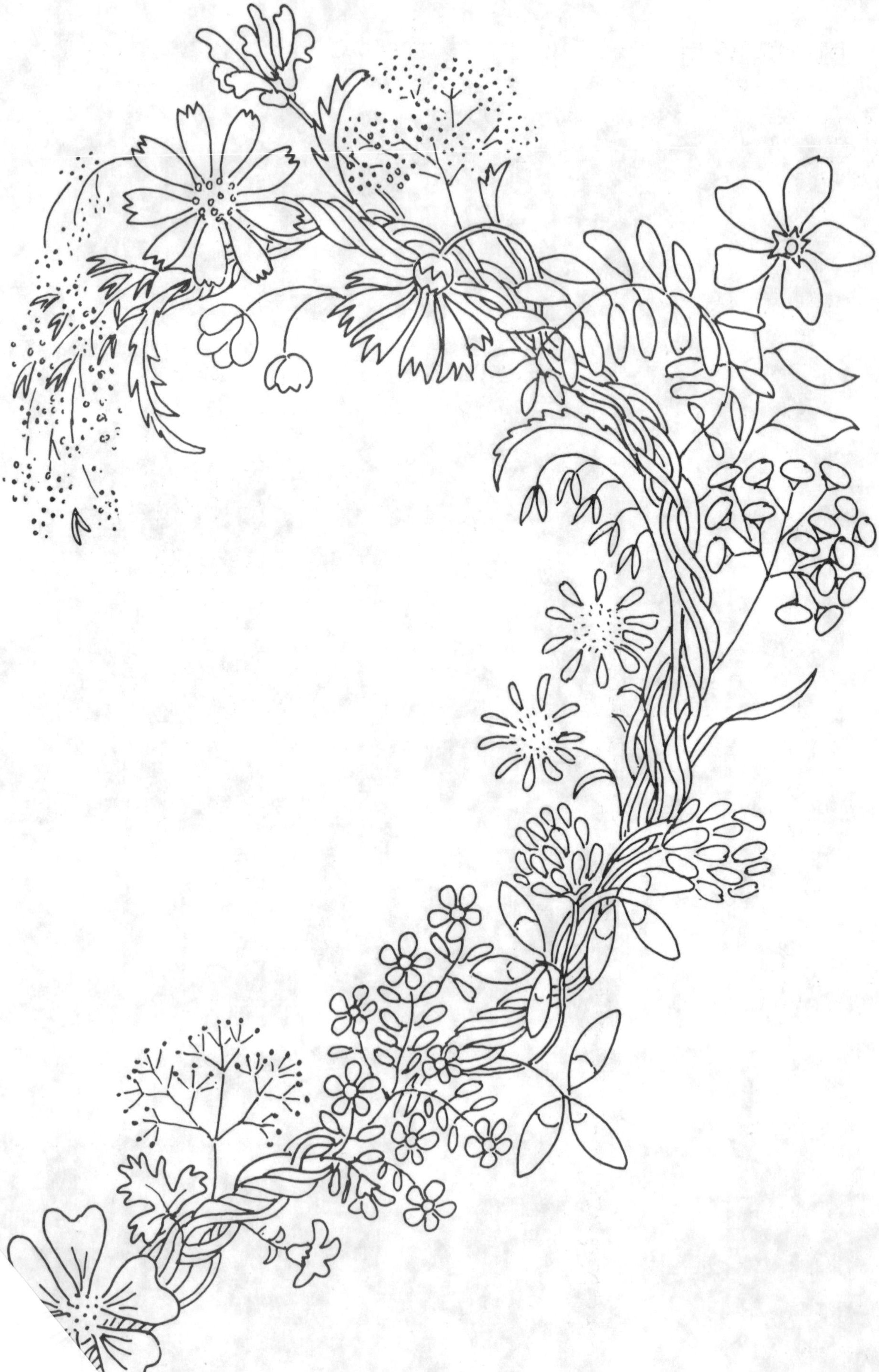